Advance Praise

"There are a thousand how-to books on hunting, but never until now has any author written a self-help book for hunters! Linden Loren's Your Hunting Healthspan *is a much needed positive for the hunting community!"*

—Jim Shockey, TV producer and host of Jim Shockey's *The Professionals, UNCHARTED,* and *Shock Therapy on the Outdoor Channel*

"Linden has a grasp on the physical and mental aspects of hunting and longevity like very few. The lessons applied will not only make you a much better hunter and increase Your Hunting Healthspan, *but they will make you a better person regardless of your age."*

—Kenton Carruth, Co-founder of First Lite

"Your Hunting Healthspan is not your run-of-the-mill book telling you to only hit the gym or eat healthier. Linden Loren's strategies for staying fit include the critical aspect of mental wellness and how outside influences affect our overall health. Whether you love to hunt or not, it's an important read for anyone interested in living their best life."

—Jana Waller, host of *Skull Bound Chronicles*

"Hunters come in all shapes and sizes, and this book has us all covered in this well-thought-out illustration of how to improve mind, body, and soul. This is not a book about seeking perfection; this is more a book about recalibrating yourself, ensuring you make the most out of your potential. Linden executes his narrative brilliantly by using real-life experiences. Anyone who has spent time in the backcountry will relate to his stories, and anyone who has not will learn from them. This is a well-thought-out insight on how to make, gain, and benefit the most from our short time on this earth. It's not just hunters who will gain from Linden's rules on gaining a better, longer, disease-free life. I would recommend this to anyone wishing to find a better path."

—Rob Gearing, Founder and Managing Director at Spartan Precision Equipment

"If you enjoy hunting and want to better the odds of having more hunting opportunities in life, Your Hunting Healthspan *is a must-read. Not only are the health-promoting strategies practical, but they are also worth the effort. Linden Loren is bringing value to the hunting community like never before."*

—Aron Snyder, owner of Kifaru

"If you care about your health and have a strong passion for hunting, then put this book on your required reading list! You will learn how to age better, prevent disease, and live a more fulfilling life while doing things you love. This book will help you navigate even the toughest times and get you back on top. In this book, Linden Loren does a fantastic job meshing his two passions: health and the outdoors."

—Sereena Thompson, creator of the Successful Hunters Course

"Linden approaches hunting from a holistic health perspective in a practical way. A wealth of knowledge to guide your mind and body toward success in the field."

—Tom Ryle, sales and marketing manager at Washington Department of Fish and Wildlife

"A uniquely interesting angle on the synergistic relationship of nature, hunting, and personal health."

—Bert Sorin, Founder of Sorinex Outdoors

"A great read for any outdoorsman looking to improve their overall health and way of life."

—Travis Glassman, bowhunter

YOUR HUNTING HEALTHSPAN

YOUR HUNTING HEALTHSPAN

73 WAYS HUNTERS CAN AGE BETTER & PREVENT DISEASE

LINDEN LOREN

Disclaimer: The information provided in this book is for information purposes only and is not intended to be a substitute for professional medical advice, prescription, diagnosis, treatment, or cure for any health condition/disease. Always seek a physician, primary care provider, or other qualified healthcare professional's advice with questions you may have regarding a health condition. Upon using any of the information contained in this book, you agree to accept full responsibility and all risks of any costs, damages, and legal fees potentially resulting from the application of any of the information provided in this book. References from peer-reviewed studies convey associations throughout the book but do not offer guarantees or absolutes. Linden Loren assumes no liability for the application of the information presented in this book.

The Food and Drug Administration has not evaluated these statements. This product (book) is not intended to diagnose, treat, cure, or prevent any disease.

Copyright © 2023 Linden Loren
All rights reserved.

YOUR HUNTING HEALTHSPAN
73 Ways Hunters Can Age Better & Prevent Disease

FIRST EDITION

ISBN 978-1-5445-4400-7 Hardcover
      978-1-5445-4398-7 Paperback
      978-1-5445-4399-4 Ebook

For my family

*For those who have advanced to the
next stage in the process of life*

For the next generation of hunters

For the hunting community

CONTENTS

Introduction 1

Chapter 1
THE FUNDAMENTALS 7
Merging Health with Hunting

Chapter 2
DESIGNED 47
Move Like a River

Chapter 3
FOCUS ON THE LONG TERM 87
Dietary Habits as a Way of Life

Chapter 4
OVERLOOKED AND UNDERVALUED 137
Better Sleep Is Natural Energy

Chapter 5
KEEP IT SIMPLE 169
Breath, Stillness, and the Environment

Chapter 6
REWIRING OUR BRAIN 215
Stay a Student and Live Simply

Chapter 7
TAKE A LOOK OUTSIDE THE BINOCULARS....247
Enjoy the Journey and Continually Improve

Conclusion 277

Call to Action 283

Acknowledgments 285

Endnotes 289

INTRODUCTION

Do you want to experience more opening days and hunting opportunities?

If you are reading this book, then you most likely replied in the affirmative. How could you not? More opening days and hunting opportunities mean more time outdoors doing what you enjoy, feeding your family nourishing meat, creating memories, and telling tales to loved ones and friends. My life has always included hunting as a way of life. Since I can remember, my parents have taken me on numerous hunts. Hence the book cover; most of my memories of my father include some form of wild game.

I want you to understand that life is too short not to pursue your passions or strive to be a better version of yourself. Both time and our health are never guaranteed. I like to hunt. I hope to be doing it for a long time, and I hope the same for you. Suppose you want to better the odds of experiencing more opening days and hunting opportunities. In that case, it may be worth it to start making better lifestyle choices in favor of your health. Let's begin with an example.

Let's say you witness a hunter who consumes whatever they please, neglects to exercise and take care of their health, yet manages to harvest a mature bull elk. Yes, this does occur. Probably more often than not. Let's skip ahead ten years, though. Finally, the hunter has twenty preference points for a Bighorn sheep tag. And this year, they finally drew this bucket list tag, but they have also recently received a diagnosis of a new disease that prevents them from participating in this hunt. Most hunters would probably be discouraged by this situation. It's possible that during the previous ten years, this disease could have been prevented.

We must realize that we can change the quality of our lifestyle choices without having an "epiphany" or even a health-related issue. It's possible to focus on the prevention side of health rather than waiting until a health limitation arises and then doing something about it. Sometimes it's too late at that point. For this reason, I urge you to take action and improve your health so that you can continue hunting. Being able to continue going on that yearly turkey hunt with your family and that deer hunt with your daughter because you have better health sounds good to me.

Vitality is not achieved by mastering only one health variable. It is an accumulation of variables or components that add up and make our bodies flourish. We may never know everything that leads to solving the equation of perfect human health, but we can always continue learning, applying, and finding more keys to this puzzle.

The decision is rather simple: adapt and improve our lifestyle choices, or raise our risk of getting sick sooner and missing our next hunt.

Let's say we experience headaches frequently. These may even affect our upcoming Whitetail deer hunt in Pennsylvania, causing us to experience frustration, sadness, anger, and other negative emotions. Our recent headache was not an accident. We created an environment within ourselves to make it home. It did not randomly appear. A stomachache after every meal, migraines once a week, extra weight gain, irritability, insomnia brought on by work stress, anxiety and depression, low energy levels all day, and frequent back pain are not random occurrences. If we don't investigate the problem to find its root cause, it can generate other issues. No matter who we are, where we come from, or how old we are, health limitations and diseases do not care. Anyone can be affected, and anything can thrive if the proper environment is created within us.

Without a doubt, the quality of our lifestyle choices and any potential genetic predispositions we have affect how healthy we are. There are, however, people with genetic anomalies whose genes are fixed and unchangeable. Either way, we can positively influence our health and life through better lifestyle choices to some degree. We may have a genetic predisposition for a disease, but that does not guarantee that the disease will manifest inside us. For example, I have a gene that expresses an increased risk for blood cancers such as leukemia. The possibility that the disease will manifest itself can be decreased if I continually make better lifestyle choices on a consistent basis, like getting enough sleep, exercising, and fasting.

Our genes do not fully determine our future. Circumstances and predispositions might affect our health; still, we must be accountable for what we allow our health to become. Have you ever been in a position where your hunt was interrupted due to poor health? Perhaps your health prevented you from going hunting at all. Hopefully, your attention is starting to focus on what these words could mean for you.

It would help if you recognized that there is already free healthcare that exists; it always has. It's called lifestyle choices such as exercising, stretching, exposure to natural light, good quality sleep, nature, a positive attitude, nasal breathing, grounding, reading, stillness, fasting, cold showers, eating nourishing foods, etc. The good news is that when we accept this idea, the healthcare we receive is solely based on our consistent effort and accountability. When we give thought to it, one of the better health insurance policies for hunters is to make better lifestyle choices.

Hunters who consistently make better lifestyle choices will enjoy happier, higher-quality lives and engage in more hunting. They will also possess greater physical, mental, and spiritual health. The key to making this sustainable is emphasizing progress more than "perfection."

It's essential to understand that many health limitations and diseases that exist may require specific prevention tools, recommendations, and treatment options that need to be considered. At the very least, though, if we incorporate the health-promoting strategies listed throughout this book, there is a good chance we might prevent and improve these health limitations and diseases to some extent. Case in point: you can improve your current health status no matter your position. Recognize that without our health, there is no schedule, no time spent with family, no retirement, no helping with conservation efforts, and no more hunting trips.

In this book, as the title suggests, I provide *73 Ways Hunters Can Age Better & Prevent Disease* that are considered investments into *Your Hunting Healthspan* account. I discuss each way in detail in each chapter and then recap the list at the end of the chapter. The pictures throughout this book illustrate a timeline as I age with personal stories and lessons learned.

All the information in this book has come from conversations with my mentors, childhood memories, creativity, client testimonials, academic background, book readings, internships, and professional and personal experiences. The references in this text do not provide guarantees; instead, they merely suggest potential relationships between various concepts.

I have not conveyed ideas for *Your Hunting Healthspan* that I am not willing to use or experiment with. I am also not a master of any of these strategies mentioned. I am also not a doctor; I am not a scientist; I am far from the most learned; I am not a registered dietician; I don't have wisdom (my teeth never came in); and I am not a therapist. I am not an expert on any topic or field, but I would be happy to refer you to someone who is. I'm just a small-town individual who happened to grow up in a hunting-loving household. An individual who also developed an interest in the field of health sciences and decided to combine the two to help hunters experience more opening days and hunting opportunities.

I hope you find this book helpful by any measure. I've found the concepts I mention incredibly valuable for my life, and others have found the same. I would be delighted if you decided to learn, investigate, and experiment with my strategies to age better and prevent disease. As you read this book, I strongly encourage you to reflect on how it could apply to your life after each reading day. Write down notes and ideas and underline things that pertain to your life.

We are born, and we will surely die; the interim is what counts. Now is the best time to recalibrate and embark on a new journey toward better health, more opening days, and more hunting opportunities.

You get to decide if you want to change your lifestyle choices. Improving your health is all on you, nobody else. Not your friends, family, or social media activists—only *you*.

I'll ask the same question again: do you want to experience more opening days and hunting opportunities?

CHAPTER 1

THE FUNDAMENTALS

Merging Health with Hunting

At 4:45 a.m., the alarm goes off. Fog from my breath instantly tells me that it will be a cold one this morning. August 24, 2019. Archery elk season here in Oregon reminds me of a morning similar to the Super Bowl. Quiet now, but it could get wild later on. Luckily, I have on my First Lite merino-wool long johns to help preserve my body heat as I lie in my sleeping bag. Getting up early in the morning out of that warm bed into the cold is not always easy. But it's a no-brainer to get out into the uncomfortable when preparing all year for this trip.

Gear put on fast to beat the coldness from sneaking in. I know I am not the only one who races the cold. Headlamp on as my third eye. Twenty-degree temps may not be chilly to some folks, but it has a nice bite right now. We rush out of camp for a nice two-mile warm-up hike to get to our desired location. I hope a good picture has been painted so far. Imagine if hunting that morning is not an option because of a health limitation such as a severe stomachache.

A stomachache that could have been prevented. Sometimes we forget that we can influence our physical body and mental outlook by making better-quality lifestyle choices.

The human body and mind orchestrate several mechanisms that allow us to carry on with our daily lives and enjoy hunting year after year. Treat the body and mind well; it flourishes. Treat the body and mind poorly; it withers away. Our true identity is our current health. And in this context, *Your Hunting Healthspan*.

Your Hunting Healthspan is the quality of your physical, mental, and spiritual health in connection with experiencing more opening days and hunting opportunities. Making better-quality lifestyle choices to improve our health increases the odds of being able to hunt more, age better, prevent disease, heal more effectively, and feel terrific during the off-season and while on the hunt.

> Here's something to think about in relation to our health. In 2008, literature suggested that 90–95 percent of cancer cases are due to environmental and lifestyle factors, while 5–10 percent are due to genetic defects.[1] Maybe we have more influence over our health than we initially thought.

We all have a huge potential to influence our *Hunting Healthspan* in the short and long term, which is one of the main reasons I am accumulating information and disseminating it to all hunters. I've been on a quest to upgrade the quality of my lifestyle choices for the last six years—from the very ideas I discuss throughout the book. If I didn't see results myself or see others succeed with these ideas,

I would not try and pay it forward. The good news is that, like the time we spend getting ready for our hunting expeditions, the season for health improvement never ends.

If we want to possess better health to experience more opening days and hunting opportunities, then being accountable and doing things differently is paramount. We could wait for that supposed miracle drug that will cure all diseases. The truth is it might never exist in our lifetime or ever. If it's ever claimed to be developed, there is a good chance of repercussions or side effects that cause other health issues. We can't rely solely on modern medicine to always bail us out. The deal of life requires us to fulfill our end of the bargain by actively living a life where we consistently try to improve our health—a prevention mindset. Modern healthcare, plus effort in making better lifestyle choices on a consistent basis to improve overall health, is a perfect combination for more vitality and more hunting trips.

BUTTERFLY EFFECT

The "Butterfly Effect" is one of the best ways to grasp the power of change that can enhance *Your Hunting Healthspan*. The following is an example of the Butterfly Effect's influence in this context:

A week of making 1 percent better lifestyle choices per day results in 7 percent better health at the end of the week. Imagine carrying out that each day for a year. I think it would be great to be 365 percent healthier by the end of the year. Therefore, even the smallest adjustments to daily choices can have a big impact in the short and long run.

Minor changes to lifestyle choices, such as decreasing phone usage before bed, can improve our sleep quality. Over time, these small changes can enhance our overall health. Which, as we can see, can pay big dividends for our physical, mental, and spiritual health by the end of the year. We can keep going after those Mule deer in Idaho if we actively seek out moments to make better-lifestyle choices each day.

Improving *Your Hunting Healthspan* will require patience. Many, including myself, are not as patient as we could be. Just because we observe others getting the desired outcomes doesn't indicate that their success came instantly. We don't see how much time, work, and perseverance it took someone to reach that point by making many small, minute lifestyle choices that got someone in that position. Make lifestyle choices for long-term progress through patience, determination, and the right attitude. These qualities can guide us on the path we seek regarding our health in the off-season and during the hunt.

LET'S BEGIN

Thoughts are more powerful than most realize in shaping our health and life. We can literally become what we think. And since all of life is a state of mind, how we think, perceive, and believe things can change our internal chemistry, either enhancing our vitality or leading us on the path toward a poor *Hunting Healthspan*. This is why there is great joy in knowing that our body, mind, and spirit can become our laboratory, where we can test out practical lifestyle-based concepts to elevate the quality of our thoughts for our health, life, and hunts.

A great steppingstone for better quality thoughts starts with accepting and saying to ourselves, "I am responsible for the quality of my thoughts and for the way my health is right now." Once that is understood, progress can begin to take a route on the path to becoming a *super hunter*.

Let's start this fantastic journey by fostering a strong thought process and indestructible moral compass to improve our character (origin of the heart) and become better-quality individuals with robust health.

Remember: without health, there is no more hunting.

Stress

In the context of this book, stress is a symptom that, depending on how we perceive it, can have a positive or negative impact on *Your Hunting Healthspan*. When we experience short-term (acute) stress levels, our breathing cadence becomes more rapid, our heart rate rises, and we start to sweat a little. All of these traits are advantageous because they enable us to act at that precise moment for whatever situation we are taking on. Many of these short-term stress responses can increase our physical and mental performance concerning the situation. For example, any of the following situations with short-term stress responses may improve performance: launching an arrow from sixty-two yards at a monster moose in Alaska, giving a presentation, putting a stalk on that Dall sheep in British Columbia, exposure to cold/hot environments, going on that first date, and sprinting to cut the distance on a giant black bear in Manitoba.

Conversely, chronic stress, sometimes termed long-term stress, is the point at which we must draw the line and say, "No more." Causes of chronic stress can derive from financial difficulties, toxic relationships, busyness, trauma, social pressures, negative media, work issues, abuse, lousy lifestyle choices/habits, family problems, and so on. Chronic stress can negatively impact many systems in the human body, from originating in the mind and manifesting in the body, where health limitations and diseases gradually begin to develop. However, there are a few strategies we can use to approach chronic stress differently.

Something to Learn > Chronic Stress

The first strategy for overcoming chronic stress is to view it as an opportunity to learn something. Start by considering why we might think it's purely bad. Maybe think of chronic stress as a chance for the body and mind to search for a better route rather than as something that is always terrible. A more uplifting path can be found if we look for it.

If we let it take over and view it to be completely bad, it can be a negative influence on our health. It may even override all the health-promoting strategies we are incorporating daily. For example, maybe we have allowed chronic stress to take residence within us due to work-related issues that we think are completely bad. Despite exercising every day, consuming nourishing foods, sleeping well, and so on, we can still experience cardiovascular problems like premature ventricular contractions (extra or skipped heartbeats) from allowing the chronic stress to take over internally because of how we think about it.

Chronic stress does not have to be an inevitable part of our lives. We can approach it differently and seek out advice from others on how to look for a positive path, such as a lesson that may be drawn from the circumstance. If we choose to, there is always something to be learned from life's challenges, difficulties, and failures that can make us better and healthier people.

Understanding the significance of chronic stress in relation to the universe is the second strategy for overcoming it. Chronic stress largely stems from thoughts and emotions related to our memory and vivid imagination. Knowing this, one may wonder, *In the larger scheme of things, is arguing with a coworker significant?* Or, *Is that expensive bill important in the big picture?* They are most likely not; I'm here to inform you. When we fully internalize that humans are the size of bacteria on earth in a solar system that is the size of a grain of sand in this infinite universe, we can start to handle everything in life more effectively.

Consider our mortality. This cycle of arrivals and departures of humans has lasted for some time. And since we are here only for a limited amount of time that is not guaranteed, I think these supposed stressors hold less power. We are tiny, and the things we deem stressful are even tinier.

Universe > Chronic Stress

Perhaps one day we will give in to that annoying chronic stress. It begins to overwhelm, engulf, and suffocate us. That's okay. Immerse yourself in the following tactics to assist you in letting go:

1. Converse with loved ones.
2. Focus on something intently in relation to nature (trees, insects, clouds, etc.).
3. Recall a joyful experience.
4. Exercise and stretch.
5. Engage in target practice.
6. Try nasal breathing.

7. Look at pictures of family members or friends who mean a lot to you.
8. Read a book.
9. Take on a new challenge.
10. Take a shower. For the last minute, make it cold.

The key is to use one or more as soon as we can to benefit us and our situation. The longer we immerse ourselves in these varying tactics, the more they help us see what really matters to us. Slowly but surely, the buildup of chronic stress can diminish over time.

Inconveniences and tragedies can play a significant role in chronic stress. It's crucial to understand that the severity of chronic stress can change based on the circumstance, intensity, and the person experiencing it. As a result, be empathetic toward people who struggle to cope with chronic stress that doesn't appear as severe to you.

At times, life may appear unjust. Realistically speaking, it might never be fair; therefore, we must make the best use of what we have. Although we may not have any control over the experiences life hands us, we do have control over how we let those experiences affect how we live.

We don't necessarily need to go through life attempting to stay out of the chronic stress storms. The focus is that when it does appear, we must equip ourselves with the skills necessary to face it head-on and survive. Similar to a bamboo tree. The bamboo tree, which can bend and is flexible, keeps itself erect and alive during a strong windstorm, whereas the stiff maple tree falls over. Be resilient in the face of ongoing hardship, adversity, and chronic stress like bamboo.

Hunters can respond to chronic stressors more efficiently with effort and ongoing practice if they view them as a chance to learn something new and acknowledge their insignificance in the grand scheme of the universe. As a result, we can better control our thoughts and emotions. We all have the capacity to handle stressful situations more effectively. We can and ought to confront these ongoing stressors head-on! Yes, you are in charge of your life.

Optimism

We usually find what we are looking for; everyone does. If we look for the good in things, we will find them. If we look for the bad in things, we will find them, whether we realize it or not. The phrase "I'm sixty-seven years of age, and it's too late to focus on losing weight to help my lower back problems," or "I'm twenty-four years of age, and I'll never be good at archery" are examples of pessimism in the hunting community. Some of us reading this may be familiar with someone who fits one of these descriptions. According to how we perceive the future, optimism is the belief that good things can happen and that they could be favorable.

Every coin has two sides. And in this instance, it appears that pessimism could be connected to worse health and that independent of our current health condition, socioeconomic status, and health behaviors (diet, alcohol, and smoking), we may have a longer life span on average if we are optimistic.[2] There is no doubt that the quality of our thoughts can have a positive or negative impact on our DNA.

Pessimism is a micro-toxin that, in low doses (for a short period of time), can be relatively safe but, in high quantities, is extremely harmful to our bodies and minds (long term). Even the relationship between being pessimistic and getting older biologically may exist.

Our internal health and how our cells function is referred to as our biological age. This is distinct from our chronological age, which refers to the duration of our existence. Although our chronological age is unchangeable and unalterable, our biological age could change depending on the quality of lifestyle choices we make. For instance, you might be fifty-two years of age chronologically but be biologically forty-six due to making healthier lifestyle choices like getting enough sleep, improving your dietary habits, exercising, and being more optimistic.

Let me give you an example of a hunting scenario where optimism is neglected: the weather. The fact that the weather wasn't "perfect" is a great opportunity for all hunters to practice optimism. We occasionally gripe that the weather prevents us from seeing or harvesting wild game the way we want. Maybe the weather is the exact opposite of what we need it to be for an optimal hunt, so be it. Prepare for the weather, but don't let it control how you feel and alter your behavior.

One of my favorite weather conditions to hunt in is when it's cold and uncomfortable out—particularly hunting black-tailed deer in the backcountry. This may be the case because it seems like my father only ever took me out in this weather. Even if I find it more mentally challenging to be in warmer weather, I accept this and don't complain or dwell on it. If I'm capable of handling unfavorable conditions, you can too.

There is a difference between talking about the weather conditions and what they are versus complaining about them. A downpour or extreme heat that makes hunting more difficult isn't a reason to complain and surrender. It's a reason to stay put and embrace it. We don't always need perfect conditions to enjoy and gain something from the hunting experience. Mother Nature most likely has something to teach us all, along with a healthy dose of humility.

Throughout our hunts, it can be difficult to remain positive. Inadequate weather, unfavorable game laws, a bow breaking, a flat tire on the way to camp, forgotten boots, missing the mark on a large bull elk, having bloody heels, the rangefinder not working, a lack of wildlife, a long journey down a canyon to retrieve our harvest, and so on. I've also been there. It's about positively progressing and expanding our perspective, not about being perfect. The process of improving as a hunter by reducing complaining and pessimism is what's important.

To improve your attitude, start by focusing on yourself, then pay attention to the outside world. Now we are making progress. What if our attitude and perspective on the circumstance are causing the issue in our lives? Portraying or suppressing negative thoughts is not the only option. Accept them and then deliberately tell yourself to replace them with optimistic and positive thinking; this works better than allowing pessimistic and negative thoughts to fester inside, manifesting into stress and sickness. Remember, we always find what we are looking for.

Self-reflect and find ways to be more optimistic and positive in various circumstances, then apply those behaviors. The sacrifices made, miseries experienced, and suffering endured by combat veterans, like my mentor Jay, so that I can have the opportunity to hunt, exercise, read books, and so on is one of my go-to reminders that helps me break the habit of complaining and being pessimistic in general. I can live a better life with fewer complaints once I keep this in mind plus, it allows me to express gratitude toward veterans every day rather than just one day a year.

A lack of optimism while complaining can prevent us from improving our *Hunting Healthspan* by making us believe we don't need to put in the effort to better ourselves. Then we wonder why life is not as enjoyable at home or in the woods as we would like it to be.

There is no return on our investment with complaining. Always making a situation seem "wrong" and ourselves "right" actually can feed our ego more. As a result, we could have an unhealthy sense of self-importance because we think we are right, which is not good. Complaining and believing we are always correct reinforces the ego and makes it harder to regulate in the long run, particularly if this happens frequently.

It is crucial to realize that regardless of our age, we can change the way we live if we so choose. It's not too late to be more optimistic and adopt a healthier lifestyle if we are eighty-four years of age. It's not too early to be more optimistic and adopt a healthier lifestyle if we are seventeen years of age. Everyone can improve their "optimistic genes." Here is how:

1. Surround yourself with other optimistic people and go-getters. In doing so, something will take place within you that seems magical. It is called "the optimism contagion," which subconsciously impacts you in favor of your thoughts and health.
2. Read books that are positive, inspiring, and uplifting.
3. Look for the good in things.

A day spent in a tree stand, field, or woods is a privilege. Be thankful that we are a part of this worthwhile lifestyle because we only get one life. Choose to employ optimism; you are the master of your attitude.

Mom, the deer slayer, with my dad in the 1980s.

The image of my mother and father captures the joy our family felt while participating in the deeply fulfilling lifestyle that hunting provides. My father set up an annual archery camp around this time, where my mother, brother, and their friends gathered. At this period, I was not yet born. However, based on what I've been told, these are some of my family's fondest recollections because archery hunting was still undeveloped and not as popular at the time. If you had met my mother, you probably wouldn't have realized that she was an avid archery black-tailed deer hunter who pursued deer with patience and a focused, clear mind.

When I was six years old, my mother jumped out of the truck after my father noticed a nice 2x3 black-tailed buck feeding a few hundred yards away in a four-year-old clear-cut. I was in the back seat at the time. To get a better view with dad, I crawled up onto the truck's back tailgate immediately. We had to stand on the toolbox to see mom because the brush was fairly high. She took the right steps foot by foot over logs through undergrowth silently and strategically, like a chess game, without breaking a twig. It was my type of entertainment—like having front-row seats to a hunting movie. I believe she was at a distance of around forty yards when she fired her first shot, which just missed the buck. At that point, the deer became attentive and moved forward cautiously because of what had happened. Then it resumed feeding. Mom is fortunate to get another chance. Within ten minutes, she gradually closes the distance to thirty yards, at which point the deer turns to face her. At this moment, we are still on the toolbox, watching this action unfold as if it were a movie. She pulls back and holds for what feels like an eternity. When it is finally released, the arrow strikes precisely behind the front shoulder. I will never forget watching the shot because I thought my heart would burst with excitement. After forty-five minutes of waiting, we joined my mother as she made her way over to fetch the deer she had just taken with her bow. One of the best days of my life, which I will always remember.

Mom brings home the deer meat, and dad brings home the bear meat—for me, this was a usual scene. Thinking about this has made me realize how fortunate I am to be a hunter. This story also demonstrates when my mother chose the positive path after shooting an arrow that missed its target. She always maintains her mental stability when dealing with setbacks since she knows all the reasons to be thankful. Fortunately for me, my parents would teach me how to start training my mind to be optimistic and to think positively later in life.

Kindness

Being kind is a fundamental human quality that is necessary for overall life satisfaction. It's a quality that includes being thoughtful, generous, and friendly. Giving and receiving kindness has advantages for both parties involved. When we are kind to others, it makes us feel good within, which promotes the health of our body, mind, and spirit. More specifically, stress levels drop, anxiety lessens, and hormones become more balanced. Even more, experiencing happiness may result from showing kindness.[3]

Unfortunately, there is still a lack of kindness in the world, and that permeates the hunting community. One of the most common situations is when male hunters criticize women for engaging in a "man's" lifestyle. When people fall into this kind of gender bias, their selfishness, pride, and poor moral compass become overwhelmed with insufficient energy to the point where it is challenging to detach from misguided thoughts, also known as internal torturing.

Perhaps we could attempt to create a new tradition of kindness with higher moral standards for the sake of the next generation of hunters. I hope women hunters realize that life is moving too fast to turn around and stop hunting because of someone else's hurtful remarks. You see, hunters, kindness is not a sign of weakness. Being unkind is weak and inhibiting, whereas being kind is an absolute strength.

Hunters can show kindness in various ways, such as sharing their last successful hunt's high-quality meat with someone who needs it more, sharing their favorite hunting area with someone, and letting their hunting partner use their knife while theirs is missing. We can also offer encouraging words to someone who is going through a tough time in life. Give compliments to people who have achieved their goals. Open doors for others. Say please, and thank you even for the little everyday tasks. When we express character traits such as these, we will most likely start a chain reaction where the individual to whom we expressed kindness then expresses kindness to another person. Whether or not they can help us, look for ways to be kind to hunters and non-hunters. One act of kindness has the potential to drastically alter the course of someone's life in a good way.

A word of advice: whether we are kind to someone doesn't depend on their physical attributes, such as amputations, stretch marks, deformities, hair loss, rashes, being overweight or underweight, varicose veins, birthmarks, acne, being short or tall, eczema, scars, or wrinkles.

Humility

When was the last time you received a nice piece of humble pie? Throughout my life, I have received a nice dose of humility several times. My father started teaching me about this quality when I was six years old. He was determined to teach me how to appreciate the concept of humility when I first started having sports success as a young child. One of the conversational pearls that has stuck with me to this day is when he mentioned that those who take the humble path frequently experience a better quality of life. At the time, I started to see the connection, but as I've become older, I can now understand what he intended to convey.

A humble person displays less ego and arrogance. A humble individual doesn't think their skills, talents, or accomplishments are better than those of others (superiority complex). They are committed to improving themselves, accepting responsibility for their mistakes, and being receptive to constructive criticism.

I'm always humbled by archery elk hunting for several reasons, such as anticipating the elk's behavior, putting patience and willpower to the test, or repeating the same error. Sharing our hunting struggles and failures with others is one approach to embracing the concept of humility. In actuality, hardly every hunt goes exactly as planned. This is why it's encouraging to hear hunters talk about difficulties they've faced, like missing a shot. Truth and authenticity are always appreciated and encouraged.

An experience that's etched into my memory occurred during the summer of 2016 on our backcountry hunt. During this hunt, I missed six shots at six different elk with my bow in one week. Never before have I come so close to giving up bowhunting. Even my older brother sarcastically said, "Alright, you're not my brother right now,"—temporarily disowning me for making so many mistakes. Luckily, in the end, my brother and his friends encouraged me to learn from my mistakes and stick with it. Through each miss, I learned something new, making me a better archery hunter. Funny to reflect on. After I returned from that trip, I created a study guide with lessons I had learned as a helpful reminder to review before future hunts. The story is not entirely full of failure, though; on the final day of the hunt, I was fortunate to harvest a beautiful 4x5.

Once it is practiced, humility helps people learn and think more effectively because they are less concerned with how they appear on the outside and more concerned with what they need to do internally to improve. Developing humility enables us to be open to learning and investigating ways to improve our lives, such as our health. These lessons we pick up out in the field serve as little teachers that help us become more mentally refined during the off-season. Even if I cannot return from the hunt with meat to put in the freezer, I still leave with new insights and lessons learned that I can apply back home. Being humble can benefit us in every aspect of life. I'm eager to swallow a bite of humility because I know it will be a win either way.

The Ego

The term "ego" is used to describe a person's sense of self-importance in relation to their thinking. Wants, anxiety, and fear, which determine a person's desired status, serve as their base. Each of us needs an ego to survive, but allowing it to run amok can result in unintended effects.

When an experienced hunter makes fun of a new hunter for wearing "lower quality" gear or not knowing certain things, that is an example of how the ego is displayed. Another example would be when a hunter tries to belittle and make fun of a non-hunter for making rude remarks. An unchecked ego can lead to entitlement, distorted thinking, and the belief that we are superior to others. If our ego becomes excessive, it can take us down a path where the odds of damaging our pride and personal identity increase if a situation doesn't go our way. When we have control of our ego, we'll be more concerned with our character than our appearance, image, and status.

By convincing us that we do not need to make better lifestyle choices, our ego can cause harm to our health. For instance, an ego can assert that "reading books is unnecessary because it is a waste of time." Reading books can actually improve the health of our brain, thinking abilities, and mental well-being. So, you can see how it can be quite difficult to choose a healthier lifestyle if we let our ego control our body, mind, and spirit. *You* are the captain; therefore, tell the ego it won't prevail today, tomorrow, or next week.

When the ego is tested, we occasionally act and say foolish things out of anger. In daily events like disagreements or arguments, anger can build over time and may set off internal chemical processes that could throw our health out of balance. In this instance, we are engaging in a self-defeating manner that gives us a false sense of contentment that we believe solves the issue.

Disagreement can exist without escalating into a heated argument.

However, if the conversation suddenly becomes an argument, there is another way to approach this situation differently. Think back on work colleagues. Have you ever argued with a coworker? To the point where it made you incredibly angry inside since it didn't go your way? This is our ego that has been challenged. The funny thing is, I think whoever decides to say, "You know what, I see your point" in an argument actually wins because they realized the argument is incredibly insignificant in the grand scheme of things. Here is how you test that theory. Recall the last thirteen arguments you have been a part of in order of date, time, location, person, and topic. There is a reason why completing this task may be difficult.

Any person who makes a similar statement is someone who is able to keep their ego in check before getting angry. You see, whoever "wins" the argument loses because they let their anger override them, fueled by their ego. So, it may feel like they "win" in the short term, but they actually lose in the long term because they were not able to get a grasp of their ego. This makes it more difficult for them to control it in the future. Similar to how when we dig ourselves deeper into a hole, it becomes more difficult to escape.

Even if we win the argument, our life typically doesn't change all that much for us thereafter. Take off in a space shuttle, for instance, and observe Earth from orbit. Now take a photo of the planet. Then, after you win an argument, take another photo of the planet. What do you suppose the distinction would be in the images? Not much, just a slight adjustment to the earth's orbit. In an argument, the person who gives up first is actually the winner. And since they have got their ego under control, they are more likely to get it under control again in the future. Bowing down first in an argument is actually a badass superpower because you own your ego. I think taking this approach is better than going the extra mile to disprove the other person's statements.

In daily life, if someone or something can make us angry, this can cause us to feel conflicting emotions, which can lead to a type of internal enslavement. We must try our best in this circumstance not to hold on to our anger. It can rot within us, bring about sickness, and lead to sadistic tendencies. With continued exposure, it may even affect how much we enjoy our hunting trip, our aim, the quality of our sleep, our capacity to choose healthy foods, the health of our cardiovascular system, the effectiveness of our workouts, the strength of our memory, and other factors. Instead, consider using different methods to release it, so it doesn't build up. These might include exercise, target practice, being in nature, taking cold showers, and nasal breathing.

Acknowledge your anger and understand that how you react can either fuel it or extinguish it. If we become aware of this and change our response, we have just won a battle with our ego. The more battles we win over our ego, the less angry we will be, and the more we will gain control.

When it comes to harboring anger, insecurities, negative feelings, envy, pride, and potentially inflated self-image, an uncontrollable ego is comparable to a fortress. What if the truth about who we truly are is hidden behind our walls? The truth, full of joy and inner pleasure, must be uncovered if we want to live a better quality of life. Knock…those…walls…down…

> Remember that even though some aspects of life are beyond our control, we always have a choice in how we react to them.

Accountability

An excellent place to start cultivating the ability to manage our ego and emotionally charged thinking is by self-reflecting and being more accountable. One can put their ego and sense of pride to the side while hunting by accepting full accountability for missing a shot at a Rocky Mountain elk in Arizona rather than blaming the gear, the weather, or the guide. That broadhead didn't work as effectively because we may have aimed our arrow poorly.

Once we become accountable for our words and actions, it is liberating because we realize we are in full control, resulting in internal peace and happiness. Blaming is relatively easy and addictive, so accountability these days is rare because we must accept actual ownership of ourselves. For instance, I used to attribute my poor performance in math class to the professor and the coursework back in college. Ironically, neither the professor nor the coursework was to blame for my poor grades. I studied once a week; thus, that was the issue. Guess how we improve a skill? We frequently engage in it. So, yeah, it was my own fault. Looking back, this makes sense when things didn't go the way I wanted in life.

Think back on the off-season and honestly examine whether you have placed blame on others for your mistakes or failures. If you have, now is the chance to make a change and grow as a person. By doing this, we put ourselves in a better position to positively impact the next generation of hunters.

Taking accountability is not only about owning up and being vulnerable to what we have said or done; it also requires effort to fix the situation or problem to the best of our abilities. It can be challenging to apologize for our words or actions since it requires great courage to admit mistakes. Just because something is difficult doesn't mean we can't overcome it. Everyone possesses the strength and capacity inside themselves to be more accountable. Step up to the plate and start being more accountable for everything you say and do. It teaches us to be honest with ourselves and moves us one step closer to a better understanding of who we really are. Making mistakes and owning them shows a sincere heart.

Using "physical reminders" is one method for increasing our capacity for accountability. Say, for instance, that we must perform 150 burpees or run a 5K every time we catch ourselves slipping up. What if you are physically incapable of choosing either option? Make the physical reminder more practical for you by modifying it, then execute. You'll probably start holding yourself more accountable afterward. It's never too late to begin to take accountability for our mistakes during the hunting season and the off-season.

Honesty

Imagine that we have lied to ourselves or others to make ourselves look better or to get out of a sticky situation. Perhaps we exaggerated how far we shot the white-tailed buck in Michigan. Ever feel "sick to your stomach" after telling a lie? We feel better when we tell the truth for a reason. Lying can cause internal stress to accumulate, which over time, can progress to other health issues like anxiety or depression. Without recognizing it, other aspects of life may become out of balance if it becomes a frequent occurrence and is not halted.

Luckily there is another option besides lying. It's called holding our character to a high standard by being honest with ourselves, friends, family, coworkers, and others. Is the diet to blame, or was it that we didn't stick with it long enough? Depending on how we respond to questions such as this, we can grow into better-quality people and live life to a greater degree.

Generally speaking, being honest with ourselves and others shows that we are sincerely engaged in life. Living a false life means making it seem like everything is joyful while we lie in the background. If this describes you, you still have time to get as far away from this way of life as you can. Start the rocket and leave right away.

To get to the base of being truthful, sometimes we have to peel back some onion-like layers. We can begin by gradually removing the layers, day by day, to see deeply within and more clearly understand the root causes of our life's dishonesty. By doing this, we may come face-to-face with an idea that serves as the foundation of our own barriers preventing the truth from being revealed—*ourselves*. No longer is it necessary to twist the truth. Here is the best part: we will have way less fear and anxiety about being exposed in front of people if we are more honest with ourselves and others. Isn't that great? I think so. We don't have to worry about the truth being exposed because it already is by being honest. That seems like a comforting path to be on, full of internal ease. In the beginning, in the middle, and the end, the truth prevails.

Examine your life for areas where you can be more truthful with others. Suppress the urge to indulge in these negative traits like lying. Attack your lies by stepping on them with the truth. When we become more honest, we get a step closer to becoming happier people. A happier person equates to better mental health and experiencing more opening days.

Respect

We must first respect ourselves. Furthermore, the more respect we have for ourselves, the more respect we can then give to others and the environment. In general, I think, at the very least, we should demonstrate greater respect for those who are different from us and the environment we are surrounded by on a daily basis, especially nature, to represent the hunting community better and serve as an example for the next generations of hunters.

As hunters, we can start by respecting the land. Know where we can hunt and where we can't. Make sure the environment is clean by picking up trash in camp. Respect the wild game pursued. Educate ourselves on the anatomy of the animal. Complete the best shot we can that includes a short expiration with less suffering. Be grateful and express thanks for the harvest that will result in high-quality meat. Make the most of its resources as much as we can (meat, organs, bones, fat, etc.). Be aware of the cultural heritage in the area we are hunting. Respect fellow hunters, their camps, and their knowledge. Make sure we are prepared both physically and mentally to respect the guides and outfitters. All these respect-related elements impact our internal health and the quality of life we experience. Less respect causes us to develop internal stress more quickly, which may eventually compromise our health in various ways.

Sometimes our hunting trips don't work out the way we expect. Other hunters may experience setbacks, such as missing the shot of a lifetime, getting hurt before a hunt, having an archery release malfunction, etc. Try to be sympathetic and say something uplifting. Being considerate of others' feelings is one of the foundational aspects of respect. Be polite and courteous, and strive to uphold your character to a high standard.

This picture is of my mother and both of my brothers out hunting before I existed.

One approach to make sure we have a chance to get the high-quality meat we want is to always practice with our tools, no matter how new, used, or old they are. In this manner, there is a higher probability of getting dialed in and making the ideal, well-placed shot.

The quality of the equipment in use at the time is one of the aspects of this photograph that merits attention. No site, rangefinder, or waterproof clothing. It's crucial to realize that we can improve our skills and boost our success in the field regardless of the equipment we use.

Listen with Intent and Be Present

Have you ever been at a hunting camp chatting with a friend when suddenly your thoughts start to stray and turn to something else, such as what you'd like to do differently on the next hunt? Yeah, me too. When I was younger, I was a victim of "blind listening." In essence, it's the illusion of listening while not paying attention to the conversation at hand and being preoccupied with something else. I can still recall the times when I wasn't paying attention when my father tried to teach me how to string my longbow or fall timber. I was instead lost in thought, preventing myself from understanding what he was saying. It's a sad way to live because I'm certain I lost out on some valuable moments.

An open door is similar to listening; it's a chance, a possibility to something greater and something to be learned. A closed door is identical to not listening, with no chance or opportunity of learning something new. As I age, it is becoming more apparent that listening with intent needs constant nurturing and effort to improve. It starts with crushing those compulsive tendencies of wanting to respond quickly. Then, doing our best to avoid emotional, fast-paced responses by slowing ourselves down internally, concentrating, being patient, absorbing, figuring things out, and then responding. A conscious uninterrupted response is a conversation worth having—sign me up for that!

As hunters, we have a lot to learn from one another about other traditions, cultures, tactics, viewpoints, and so forth. In the off-season, we can relate to and learn from people by actively engaging in conversations at home, at work, at events, and when traveling. In every situation, listening can help us develop as humans and improve our character. One way to become better at listening is to focus on being in the present.

When you are focused on the slow, inch-by-inch stalk of a pronghorn in Wyoming and not worrying about the phone call you need to make for work when you get home, you are being present and living in the moment. You are fully present in the current moment and intensely focused on each step you take, experiencing every second of the pursuit. That means you can control your body and mind by being totally present.

On an annual basis, most of us spend more time not hunting than we do hunting. Therefore, in the off-season, there is more time to be better at being present. Reducing our memories of the past, noticing how our thoughts and emotions relate to our surroundings, multitasking less, letting go of our future fantasies, and appreciating the present moment are a few ways we can improve our ability to be present. When at home, at work, on vacation, etc., consider all of these factors.

To be able to embrace a moment or task with our complete attention without straying off course is possible. Start by adopting a consistent habit of total focus. Once we are actually in the present, overthinking will decrease—better mental health.

Dad bear hunting with a timid, young me in the early '90s.

I enter the picture at this point. With experience as a professional bear guide in Alaska, bear hunting was my father's area of specialty. The public land close to our home was full of black bears, so he knew it like the back of his hand. This photo was a yearly occurrence because there weren't many bear hunters in that area.

One advantage of being able to go hunting is that it helps to encourage us to be more present. Real life can be experienced to a greater extent when there are fewer artificial distractions. The trick is to return from our hunting trip with our upgraded skills.

This image also reminds me of the next generations of hunters. It is crucial to instill in them the value of listening with intent and being present since doing so will enable them to build the kind of life they genuinely want when they get older. Listening with intent and being present is a superpower.

Self-Awareness

Imagine a society in which everyone was conscious of their own actions and the reasons behind them. It seems simple when you read it for the first time. However, it could be more difficult than one originally anticipates to become more self-aware in life. When we are aware of our thoughts, emotions, and actions in relation to how we live, we are said to be self-aware.

When we frequently do the same thing and expect different results, self-awareness enables us to examine ourselves to make a change. For instance, self-awareness enables a person to be more disciplined and organized once they recognize that the reason they don't feel confident during their annual deer hunt may be because they didn't practice with their bow before the hunt. Finding out why we haven't been able to lose that additional body fat and get leaner even though we exercise and take lots of supplements is made easier by increasing our self-awareness. It aids in our understanding that the reason we may be in a bad mood, lose our temper easily, can't concentrate, and procrastinate may be related to the poor-quality sleep we received the night before. Developing self-awareness enables us to realize how our ability to make decisions might be impacted by the quality of the food we bring to our hunting camp. Consuming processed foods with less-than-ideal ingredients may upset our digestive system, impair our ability to think clearly, and affect how we put a stalk on that enormous black bear.

To understand what and why we do certain things or why things happen and don't happen, we could ask ourselves a variety of questions. Why do we enjoy hunting, we might wonder. Is it because the meat is so good? To maintain traditions? Why do we prefer bow hunting over rifle hunting or the opposite? Is it because we want a new challenge, or is it something our family supports? Spend some time thinking about the reasons behind the choices we make. Do they follow the advice of others? Do they come from our desires naturally? Self-awareness enables us to reflect on and understand ourselves. It helps us reflect on the things that really matter when it comes to our thoughts, emotions, and related actions. We can ask ourselves similar questions in many areas of our lives besides hunting.

Life is a game of self-awareness and recognizing where we direct our day-to-day attention. This idea is crucial for maintaining our mental wellness. Mental health depends heavily on input—what our brain processes as a result of exposure to information and the environment, including what we are seeing, hearing, and perceiving. The type of input one is allowing to enter their head could impact their feelings of anxiety, stress, or depression.

Constantly browsing through social media on our phones and watching/listening to the news on TV are just a few typical examples of input we need to be self-aware of. Both are capable of shifting our thoughts, emotions, and behavior. For instance, regular television viewing alone may be associated with verbal memory decline in the long run.[4] As a result, when we consume media or the news, whether through reading, watching, or listening, things inside of our brains and minds may change, potentially affecting our health and well-being. Staying informed in moderation is excellent, but we should exercise caution while using these tools excessively. By undermining logic, deductive reasoning, and interpersonal communication in real life, social media and television can both provide a distorted perception of life.

Social media isn't all terrible; it can be a great resource for learning, finding inspiration, and improving oneself. It's a fantastic way to meet new mentors who can give us the skills we need to better ourselves and our life. Social media is also advantageous since it gives the hunting community a better opportunity to band together and defeat legislative initiatives intended to end wildlife conservation. If you want to contribute to protecting wildlife and fisheries, check out Howl for Wildlife, an online platform that provides resources for hunters and anglers to unite and take action!

It's important to remember that the quality of the content on social media platforms can have a variety of impacts on us. So, try to look at and watch things that are uplifting, inspiring, and positive. Too much low-quality content can harm our mental health and mood and influence who we become. Even comparing our hunting success to that of others can create expectations that divert attention from ourselves, which can subsequently create jealousy, a lack of joy, and FOMO (fear of missing out). The key is to remember to put our own needs first to improve our circumstances and to retrain our brains to be excited for other hunters.

The next step in utilizing social media wisely is to examine the total time spent using these applications by going to the settings on our phones. If it seems to be eating up too much time away from our goals, something may need to change. Using set periods of the day and a usage cap is an approach many people find helpful for managing their social media time. For instance, we can indulge without going overboard by checking social media apps at 12:00 p.m. and 6:00 p.m. each day for a specific amount of time, such as fifteen minutes. This way, we can maintain moderation, discipline, and control by setting a specified time of day and cutoff time. Using social media strategically can help us avoid developing an addiction and overindulging at the wrong times, which could have an adverse effect on our sleep, behavior, energy, and mental health.

If we still find ourselves overindulging too much, perhaps every once in a while, we could try replacing social media time with reading a hunting book, creating art, stretching, sharpening our broadheads, working toward goals, conversing with others, target practice, cleaning our garage, improving our relationship with our significant other, exercising, cleaning our gun, or working on fun projects. If periodic replacement is not appealing, we could improve the quality of the media we watch on our phones and even the TV. Maybe consider utilizing your phone to network, help others, and learn new things while viewing uplifting hunting-related TV shows.

One of my favorite strategies for limiting my tech usage is to reflect on whether I earned my occasional TV and social media time by successfully completing my daily tasks (exercising, eating well, working hard, etc.). If we set up social media time as a reward for being disciplined, we set the stage for practicing self-control in other aspects of our life. For instance, I promised myself I couldn't go archery hunting until this book was finished once I started writing it. With this in mind, it was easier for me to apply consistent effort for the next three years. Earning anything through hard work usually increases self-confidence and improves mental wellness.

We are essentially wandering around aimlessly when we are ignorant of what impacts our own thoughts, emotions, and actions in relation to how we live life. This is why it's crucial to challenge ourselves daily in each of these aspects. Here are a few of my preferred techniques for raising self-awareness:

1. **Walk or sit in nature:** less artificial distraction for self-reflection and establishing perspective.
2. **Stillness:** be more present, look for our causes of ignorance, and reprogram our minds.
3. **Exercise/Martial Arts:** face challenges and adversity and become more alert and focused.
4. **Reading books:** critical thinking and understanding of the world around us are enhanced.
5. **Traveling (new experiences):** broaden our sense of living and the preciousness of life.

By using these techniques to observe ourselves, we can determine the validity of our thoughts, emotions, and actions, which helps us make smarter choices and live life the way we want. We have the chance right now to gather ourselves and recalibrate our internal state. Once the right instinct through self-awareness starts to grow, we will feel incredibly empowered and ready to take on the world. We'll discover that self-awareness enables us to maximize the positivity and beauty of each and every minute of this life. It's a terrific tool for putting us on the road to improved mental health, a better quality of life, and experiencing more opening days and hunting opportunities.

A young deer eating cantaloupe out of my hand!

It's essential to expose kids to nature to maintain strong mental health and self-awareness. There are no artificial distractions, such as television, cell phones, game consoles, or other media. They have the chance to become fully present and immerse themselves in their surroundings.

When I was younger, my family and I frequently went fishing for half-pounders on the Rogue River. On one of these trips, we decided to sit and have a picnic. Soon after, a young doe decided to come out from the thicket and join us. My mother tossed some cantaloupe in her direction. Slowly, the deer made her way over to it and ate it. My mother threw her way more, and the deer returned for seconds. Then, my mother subtly leaned over and told me to gently and quietly take her a piece of cantaloupe by hand. I proceeded to walk over with the cantaloupe very cautiously, and she began to eat it out of my hand. It was quite the experience for everyone.

When I think back to many of my hunting memories and experiences, such as a stalk on a mature bull elk or carefully handing the cantaloupe to the doe, it seems as if time was able to slow down and stand still for just a moment. The memory of each scenario is so clear. Every thought, choice, and action counted. Immersing ourselves in the present and being self-aware of our thoughts, emotions, and actions is a key to developing clarity and living life the way we want.

Neutral Mindset

A neutral mindset means that whenever something good or bad happens, it simply happens. It is what it is. It's relatively easy to be happy when things are going well but just as easy to get down when the opposite happens. Here is where there is a chance to change how we approach certain situations and look at them from a different point of view.

Cultivating a neutral mindset is about not becoming too absorbed in one direction, positive or negative. One extreme to the next can feel overwhelming, as we may become more influenced by our thoughts and emotions rather than reflection and action. When something "not according to plan" happens, we tend to fight back and obsessively respond rather quickly. Instead, we could merely observe them. They often hurt less the longer we watch.

A positive mindset can be beneficial, and it generally appears like a good way to approach most situations. When confronted with a substantial challenge, it can, however, set up a sneaky trap that can catch us off guard and allow negative thinking to infiltrate and feel overwhelming.

Having a neutral mindset teaches us to become better at accepting the things that don't go our way in life and then choosing what to do next. If we allow our minds to be consumed by negative situations, they might seem heavier and even make us feel worse. An individual with a neutral mindset does not dwell on what is wrong. Instead, the person acknowledges whatever is going wrong and attempts to deconstruct the issue to determine the next move systematically. Consider the following scenario: while in camp, our hunting pants unintentionally bump up against a broadhead in our quiver, causing a substantial portion of our pants to tear. Without dwelling on it, someone with a neutral mindset would accept that this incident occurred. Then they would begin to plan improvements, like weaving the pants back together using flagging tape, 550 cord, or duct tape.

Consider how we can best use the resources at hand. Think about the bigger picture; we are in charge. Either we can dwell on what went wrong and let it consume us, or we can accept it and decide what to do next. How we react can harm our outlook on the future if we allow ourselves to become overly consumed by the lows or even highs that life will undoubtedly bring. Having a neutral mindset can aid in removing delusion, bias, and falsehood and lead to greater levels of happiness. It makes it possible for us to stop focusing on setbacks.

In essence, we can move ahead or backward with a conscious state of choosing when we put our mindset in neutral. Accept that good and bad things will happen to us while we strive to enhance our health and quality of life. No matter what, keep pushing forward.

Love

Humans are hardwired for social interaction. We are, by nature, social beings that yearn for community, belonging, and love. The benefits of developing strong relationships are numerous. In unexpected ways, love and health are connected, such as through deep relationships with family, friends, and significant others. A healthy relationship could potentially improve happiness, reduce anxiety, boost drive, lower stress, boost energy, lessen depression, improve sleep quality, control emotions, and other positive outcomes.

Healthy relationships with others are tremendously valuable because they allow us to joke around, act foolish, laugh, smile, and even cry with one another. It's what enables us to express the innate qualities we are born with and connect on deeper levels, both of which are necessary to enjoy a better quality of life. Without a doubt, the types and quality of interactions we have with other people can have a positive or negative impact on our health. In this context, I specifically discuss the elements that can lead to a successful significant relationship and how our health relates to it.

When a significant relationship between two people builds and grows year after year, their energies become intertwined and stronger. Being aware of the ½ + ½ = 1 principle is one method to grow a relationship. This describes two parts that come together to form a whole. Why is this principle helpful for love to flourish? The efficiency of two halves combined exceeds that of each half acting alone. Each of you is an equal team member; neither of you is better than the other. So, a significant other is a close teammate who helps us on various levels that we couldn't do on our own. Once this is understood, we begin to realize that true love is a shared and profound rooted connection with another individual that can improve our physical, mental, and spiritual health. As I have come to know, some of the characteristics for enhancing a relationship with a significant other are when *both* people are encouraging, honest, accountable, kind, patient, slow to anger, driven, unselfish, and communicate with openness. True love between two people who exhibit these characteristics is an absolute blessing.

Consistently making an effort is another aspect of maintaining a relationship's health. It all comes down to balance. Spend time engaging in your favorite activities, such as hunting, and spend time with your significant other partaking in shared interests. When we are out of balance due to the busyness of work, to-do lists, and other demands, a relationship is sometimes one of the first things to fall by the wayside. Understanding this can help us to see why investing time, effort, and love in our significant relationship as we do in our friendships, hunting excursions, work, home improvement projects, and vacations will improve the relationship's quality over time.

How can one begin putting in the extra effort? Ask your significant other how you can improve as a teammate for them first. This ought to set you off to a good start, especially if this question is asked regularly. Then plan at least two to three dates per month. Get creative. Go out to dinner, chat over coffee while gazing at a lake, shoot pistols, travel, run together, take an art class, etc. This is crucial, especially for parents, who frequently focus solely on their children and neglect their relationship. A significant relationship is like a plant that needs to be watered. It needs daily watering (effort) from *both* people to grow and thrive and avoid withering away. Bear in mind:

> Love your significant other not because you have to but because you get to.

Always look for ways to improve your role as a significant other. By putting effort in, we can strengthen our relationship every day. Help them with housework, openly communicate and be honest, listen more intently, go on dates, take better care of ourselves, thank them for supporting our hunting endeavors, etc. We will be able to enjoy life, have better health, and go on more hunting trips if we fill our hearts with love for our significant other. In the short and long run, a happy and mentally healthy significant relationship is more valuable than material possessions, money, or fame. My wife is, and always will be, the best and luckiest thing to ever happen to me.

Ways #1–16 to Age Better and Prevent Disease

1. Adopt the prevention mindset for health.
2. Look at chronic stressors as an opportunity to learn something new and realize they are insignificant in the grand scheme of the universe.
3. Be more optimistic.
4. Minimize complaining.
5. Display more kindness.
6. Show more humility.
7. Control and minimize your reactive ego and pride.
8. Be fully accountable for everything you say and do. Apologize when wrong.
9. Be more honest.

10. Be more respectful to people and the environment.
11. Listen with intent and avoid "blind listening."
12. Be more present with your body and mind.
13. Employ more self-awareness regarding your thoughts, emotions, and actions.
14. Put your mindset in neutral.
15. Provide support and love to your family and friends.
16. Love your significant other not because you have to but because you get to.

CHAPTER 2

DESIGNED

Move Like a River

A river is typically healthier and more vibrant than a stationary pond because of its constant movement. Like a river, our physical bodies are designed to move and be physically active. Before we dive into the many things related to physical activity, I want to remind you that the ability to move, in general, is something to be incredibly grateful for. Never take physical movement for granted; it's a privilege.

Being grateful for the ability to move reminds me of my uncle, whom I'm named after. At the age of eighteen, my uncle Linden became paralyzed from the waist down after a tragic car accident. Linden was a charismatic, driven individual who loved hunting. If someone appreciated life after a severe accident, it was him. When I was young, he instilled an invaluable amount of perspective on life and existence. One of those perspectives was how much of a privilege it is to move. He would constantly urge me to make the most of my physical capabilities, especially because some people are physically incapable of moving at all. Due to the minimal arm movement he had following the injury, my uncle could utilize a wheelchair. Despite his physical limitations, he was more successful than many people, with much more physical capabilities in the areas of family, education, and fulfillment. Looking back, what my uncle accomplished during his lifetime is quite astounding.

Like my uncle Linden, it's important to be thankful for our physical abilities both in the off-season and while on the hunt. It is a privilege to be able to move, whether we do so with a wheelchair, on our feet, or with our hands. Move, push, and utilize your physical abilities as much as you can.

This picture depicts my father taking another bear on our property behind the house, and me timidly sitting nearby.

Looking back, I realize how fortunate I was to grow up in a location where hunting was accessible just behind our home. My father, and eventually I, had a lot of hunting opportunities because our property backed up to public lands. This image makes me think of how my father constantly stressed the value of using our physical abilities. There was always something to do when we were living on this property. My father used to often make me work as a youngster, especially when I got into trouble, by having me bring cut wood into the house, dig holes for posts, and move stones for masonry. These activities assisted my father then, but, more importantly, now serve as special memories between my father and me. Looking back, those times together were incredibly precious.

TRAINING

There are many different subcategories of physical activity. One well-known method is exercise. Fitness centers and people starting new workout routines in the new year are typically linked to exercise. There is no denying the benefits of exercise for our health and happiness. I want to emphasize training as another method of defining physical activity in this context, though. Training is defined as physical activity that increases our heart rates, causes us to sweat, keeps us in shape, and, most importantly, is focused on long-term goals. Exercise and training are different primarily in that training is more intentional and has a set, consistent plan that is intended to achieve a long-term goal. Any type of movement can be included, such as bodyweight movements, stationary machines, hiking, lifting weights, and other activities. As long as there is a purposeful motive, a plan, and a long-term goal in mind, this type of physical activity can be referred to as training. The following are some reasons why hunters may want to consider regular training:

Potential Benefits of Consistent Training	
Decrease chronic stress	Balance blood sugar
Improve coordination	Improve bone density
Increase productivity	Enhance brain function
Minimize anxiety	Increase physical strength
Enhance your mood	Increase happiness
Balance hormones	Improve posture
Increase endurance	Improve balance
Improve the quality of sleep	Improve circulation and heart health
Decrease body fat	Improve skin health
Increase concentration and focus	Improve emotional stability
Help us feel calmer	Improve flexibility
Improve lean muscle mass	Improve memory
Improve gut health	Minimize depression

What if we saw a TV commercial for a pill that could provide all of those benefits? Many people would probably be eager to get their hands on it, I bet! Consistent training can increase *Your Hunting Healthspan* on various physical, mental, and spiritual levels. Without a doubt, it is a fantastic tool for maintaining our biological youth.[5]

It's wonderful to see that as time passes, more hunters are training for the physical and mental preparation required to get ready for their hunts. This is a great trend to witness since it makes it more likely that they will experience the possible health benefits indicated earlier, and as a result of better health, they may experience more opening days and hunting opportunities. As more and more hunters understand the connection with their fitness, feeling better prepared for their hunt, and improving their physical and mental wellness, there is undeniably positive momentum rising. But I also notice that many hunters are not committed to training because of things like:

1. Previous injuries or physical limitations
2. Not knowing how to start
3. Not having the time
4. Having difficulty staying consistent

Training may be neglected in these circumstances and with good reason. There is hope for people who fit into any of these categories; just follow me.

My own experience has taught me that it is difficult to deal with the mental anguish and frustration of a physical injury or limitation. Fortunately, there is a solution to this that still allows us to train. It is referred to as a modification. Modifications are training movements that are used as a substitute for a movement that we are unable to perform but it achieves the same result. A training specialist can help us modify the appropriate movement pattern for our specific needs. Look around your community or online for someone with experience in this field. By modifying training movements to our unique needs, we can still train to some extent. It is possible to accommodate conditions ranging from shoulder injuries to hip replacements and knee discomfort to back pain to physical impairment.

I can speak from experience when I say that for numerous years I modified training movements for a friend who, due to a history of shoulder injuries and surgeries, could not pull her bow back or blow dry her hair. She can now blow dry her hair, shoot arrows easily, and even perform strict pull-ups. Regardless of our physical state, we can train to some degree and accomplish what we set out to do with meticulous planning, effort, persistence, and patience.

Don't know how to start? Here is how to begin training. Today, walk for a mile or complete twenty-five pushups. Not next Monday, or next week, or the first day of the following year. Right, this very day as you read these words. It's that simple. It appears to be more of a burden than it actually is because it is addictive and it's easy to relax and not exert ourselves. We are extremely good at coming up with excuses, and there is no true incentive to do so (more on this shortly).

Get creative and work with what you've got. Maybe perform one minute of bicep curls and shoulder presses using a one-gallon water jug. Carry those paint buckets around your house for four minutes or until you start to sweat. You could also do a five-minute glute bridge hold while lying on your back in the living room. Here is a straightforward weekly schedule that you can use. Go for a fifteen- to thirty-minute walk before work on Monday, Wednesday, Friday, and Sunday, depending on your schedule. Perform one set of one to two minutes of bodyweight movements like push-ups, squats, sit-ups, step-ups, or lunges on the other days. Use the movements I've just provided or come up with something entirely new, then perform them every other day. That's a simple way to start.

When you are ready to challenge yourself more, you can further advance the movements, time frame, and so forth. We don't have to go to a gym to train to become healthy. Moving our body and training can occur in any place regardless of equipment, whether on the road, in a trailer, at home, in a hotel, or outside. For instance, I squeezed in my train ing sessions using a kettlebell at the bottom of the parking garage at the hospital where our son was delivered.

Being the role model the next generation of hunters needs means stepping outside of our comfort zone and pushing ourselves, especially when we don't want to, and have come up with every excuse in the book not to. Wouldn't it be nice to enjoy the potential health benefits mentioned earlier, be more proud of ourselves, make daily life activities feel more manageable, have less regret, and experience more opening days and hunting opportunities? If you said yes, you need to start training immediately.

I'm guilty of saying, especially when I was younger, "I don't have time," which is a common response from many when encouraged to train. We can still fit in our training sessions even if we have a packed schedule seven days a week if we are strategic and disciplined. Everyone gets the same number of minutes each day, despite popular belief. As a result, we don't necessarily need to find time; we just need to make time. The key is to develop a plan despite the demands of work, home, children, and other obligations. Everyone can make time to train.

It's crucial to remember that training can be as easy as performing bodyweight movements around our home or workspace. Maybe perform three minutes of lunges in the office break room during lunch, or spend a few minutes rowing intervals before work. Daily training doesn't have to be at the level of running a marathon every day. Think simple. Just figure out how you can move and work out to some degree each day based on your personal needs, goals, and daily schedule. Some movement is better than no movement.

Out of all the challenges I've described, I think maintaining a consistent training regimen is the one that hunters struggle with the most. The reality is that consistency has always been the cornerstone of success for many decades. Consistency does not mean starting the year off with a gym visit only to stop several months later. No matter what time of year it is, staying consistent ensures that we are still involved in active training and crushing goals. Fortunately, I have an extremely effective method for maintaining consistency with training. And I will go into great detail about that. Purpose-driven training is what it is termed.

Purpose-Driven Training

Shifting gears and changing our incentive to become purpose driven is a useful tool that allows us to stay focused and train consistently. If it feels like you can never achieve the fitness results you want, think about using this tool.

Self-reflection is the first step toward finding a purpose-driven reason for your training. Identify your reason for training. When I ask people this question, they frequently respond that their reason for training comes from their family, children, friends, health, or appearance. "I want to train so I can keep up with my kids," for instance. When their objectives are based on these things, some people can succeed. Nevertheless, many people see inconsistency inserting itself into their daily routines. I realize that the reason behind this has nothing to do with how much love they have for their family and kids. The issue I've discovered is that they still don't train for themselves.

I want to challenge you to think about a hobby or activity you want to continue doing for a long time. Something that makes you happy, like hunting. Once you've chosen your favorite hobby or activity, keep it in your mind to serve as the specific reason you train consistently. Let me explain.

At some point during my coaching career, I noticed that those who experienced the most consistent results did so for a particular reason, such as training for a specific hobby or activity. I am aware of folks who focus on training for marathons, hunting expeditions, mountaineering, weightlifting contests, baking, arrow fletching, photography, etc. You'll notice that not all of those hobbies and activities, like baking, are regarded as being physically demanding. This is when the intriguing part of the purpose-driven training tool starts.

What I've observed from people who have thought about and identified what they love to do is that it can include anything they actually enjoy, whether or not it is physically related. You could literally use your passion for painting as the purpose-driven reason you train consistently. Consistent training results in better health, which translates to more years of painting. That sounds good if you enjoy painting and want to do more of it, doesn't it?

Use your love of hunting as the specific reason for training consistently if you enjoy it a lot. Suppose that you enjoy white-tailed deer hunting. That would mean you would train consistently to enjoy more white-tailed deer hunting in the future. When you consistently train for a purpose-driven reason, such as white-tailed deer hunting, you may find that you lose weight, build muscle, reduce stress, and have other health benefits without even realizing it. Five more years or fifteen more years of white-tailed deer hunting—which would you prefer?

It's okay if hunting isn't your favorite hobby. Ask yourself what hobby or activity truly brings you joy and that you want to continue doing for a long time with improved health. Then, train consistently for that specific reason. This is one way to be dangerously consistent with training.

How do we know if we choose the right purpose-driven reason to train for ourselves? We maintain consistency. Whatever we want consistency to mean, it can. It could imply that we work out three, five, or more times each week, etc. For me, it means every single day.

I like to visualize a Rocky Mountain elk at the top of a steep mountain staring down at me and saying, "I knew you weren't fit enough," or the thrill I experience when I see a mule deer staring over a ridge at me. I no longer take days off from training after adopting this purpose-driven reason (backcountry hunting). That doesn't mean I complete a thousand repetitions of a movement each day, but it sure means I work out each day to some degree. Since I've done this, I've started to experience many of the health benefits I've always wanted, and I'm also developing more self-discipline in other facets of my life.

Always remember that you do not need to train for hours on end every day. You might only work out for ten minutes on certain days and an hour on other days. For your lifestyle, make it manageable and maintainable. Try to train at the same time of day for each session, no matter how many days and for how long you decide to be consistent, so that it develops into a solid habit. Like brushing our teeth, it develops into a lifelong habit.

When you enter your garage, living room, training facility, trailer, hotel room, etc., have your purpose-driven reason in the back of your mind to help you stay focused on the "why" of what you're doing. The results you've been seeking will start to emerge and feel amazing once you've determined what that purpose-driven reason is for you. By training on a consistent basis, you'll finally reach your goals, improve your health, and extend the duration of your involvement in your preferred hobby or activity. Here are some reasons why it's essential to consistently train:

1. Minimizes health limitations that prevent us from hunting. Better health means experiencing more opening days and hunting opportunities.
2. Prepares us for the physical and mental demands of our hunt.
3. To honor the gift of movement, some cannot train to the same degree as us due to physical/mental limitations. It's a privilege to be able to move. Show gratitude accordingly.
4. To set a good example for the next generation of hunters.
5. Instills self-discipline and creates good momentum for making better lifestyle choices.
6. Make veterans happy by demonstrating to them how we are improving ourselves with the freedom they have given us.
7. Tomorrow is never guaranteed, so make the time to experience how great this body and mind can feel when we improve it. One life is all we get.

My mother holding me at early-season archery camp.

Every year, my parents would invite family and friends to an early-season archery camp. I'm really appreciative that my parents took me to this great environment with its trees, wildlife, nature, and space to move about. Even today, these remain some of my fondest memories.

In my opinion, exposing the next generation of hunters to the outdoors as much as possible can dramatically alter their life's course in a very positive way. Not just to have the chance to engage in physical activity in a wonderful setting but also to express their imagination, creativity, and capacity for skill-building. After my mother had finished her afternoon of deer hunting, this photo was taken, complete with face paint. I was obviously too young to go hunting by myself at this age, but I sneaked around camp with my toy bow and pretended I was hunting with my parents, shooting rocks, stumps, and whatever else I could find. I enjoyed my time at camp because there was always something going on, something to do, and ample space for me to move around. This photo of my mother and I shows how much we enjoy it.

TRAINING FOR HUNTING

Let's say that our purpose-driven reason to train is hunting. And we are ready to increase the level of our training and workouts. Maybe we want to go beyond what I suggested earlier, like walking a mile or performing push-ups for two minutes. There are a few options to consider in this situation.

First, decide where you would train the majority of the time. If you want to train at home, looking online for home workout programs could help you take your workouts to the next level. There are many options available. Look for the ones that include tutorials on how to perform the movements properly to prevent injury, as well as modifications in case of a prior injury or physical limitations, to make sorting through them easier. Joining a program that provides both of these features will probably benefit you.

The ability to follow a set routine with an online workout program is really advantageous if we don't want to think about what to do. They take the uncertainty out of what to do. I am familiar with several people who have taken this route and followed an online workout program at home with great success.

We also have the option of doing bodyweight programs or programs that call for equipment, depending on our preferences. The benefits of investing in our own workout equipment are numerous.

We don't need to rely on other facilities for training, which is a huge benefit in the long run. And we have a remedy if a gym or training facility closes or is closed for an extended length of time.

Let's say you choose not to train at home. Perhaps a gym or training facility would be more of your style. Local gym memberships give you access to a variety of training options. If you want to enroll in a fitness class where someone who is more qualified leads you through the workout and makes sure you perform the movements safely, this is a great option. In addition to taking classes, you can also utilize the equipment to train on your own at a gym. For this choice, you can still choose an online workout program that provides you with more direction and equipment-required workouts you can do at the gym.

If you train at home or in a gym but want specific suggestions for movements that are more closely tied to the needs of hunting, you're in luck. I have a list of movement categories for hunting that contain various options that can make our hunting experience more manageable, elevate our performance, and lead to better health. More opening days and hunting opportunities result from improved health.

When it comes to training, many movement patterns can benefit hunters. And since all hunters have individual needs and goals in training, I encourage you to explore other movement options, not just the ones I list. In light of this, I've created six categories of movements that most hunters could find useful to think about and use. There are common movement patterns and physical demands made during all sorts of hunting. In the field and off-season, a hunter's physical health may be improved by engaging in the following types of movement:

1. Foot Speed
2. Grip Strength
3. Aerobic Capacity
4. Midline Support
5. Leg Strength
6. Rotator Cuff Stability

Foot Speed

At anytime throughout our hunt or in life in general, if we trip and fall, we must quickly recover our feet to avoid injury. Realistic scenarios where a hunter might recover and catch themselves to prevent an accident or trip, and develop a new health limitation due to slow foot speed, include crossing a log, skinning wild game, and walking in the snow or rain. Foot speed helps us change directions, which increases agility and reaction time in the field. The likelihood of suffering an injury from a fall and slow foot speed rises with age. To lower the risk of falling, we must take proactive measures to speed up our feet. Increasing our foot speed could extend the years of hunting we experience considering different terrain variables are common when hunting in the woods.

Examples of movements to improve foot speed:

- Ice Skaters
- Lateral Box Jumps/Steps
- Jumping Lunges
- Ladder Work
- Jump Rope
- Cone Drills

Grip Strength

It's likely that we will have to carry or drag something heavy at some point during our hunting adventures. Gaining grip strength increases our ability to carry heavy objects, such as a large duffle bag, equipment to our tree stand, our bow while walking, a harvested deer over a ravine, and an elk hindquarter as a friend wraps a game bag around it. These examples of dragging, holding, and carrying demonstrate how each action—which can all occur during a hunt—requires a strong grip. Handling these situations more effectively allows for less strain, preserved energy, and saved time. As we age, having a stronger grip results in fewer functional limitations and improved health.

Examples of movements to improve grip strength:

- Strict Pull-Ups
- Farmer's Carry
- Rows
- Kettlebell Swings
- Deadlifts
- Rope Climbs

Aerobic Capacity

Our conditioning shape is described by our aerobic capacity. Due to efficient blood and oxygen transmission throughout our bodies, the more developed our aerobic capacity is, the more effectively our respiratory, cardiovascular, and muscular systems will function. Recall the day you ran up a mountain in a rush to catch up to a world-record deer. Were you too exhausted to collect yourself and launch an arrow at that world-class buck at forty-three yards? We will have a stronger buffer to deal with those situations if our aerobic capacity is improved. Being in good conditioning shape enables us to improve a plethora of health benefits, including improved self-confidence, increased mental clarity, and better sleep. Now is the time to put ourselves in an advantageous position to handle those oxygen-taxing hunting situations more effectively.

We can considerably increase our aerobic capacity by mixing low, moderate, and high-intensity training sessions with various bodyweight movements, resistance, and conditioning equipment. Because Concept 2 machines boost all-around strength and endurance and can strengthen our mental toughness, I frequently include them in my workouts.

Examples of ways to improve aerobic capacity:

- Running/Hiking (aim for inclines)
- Swimming
- Biking
- Concept 2 Row Erg
- Concept 2 Ski Erg
- Concept 2 Bike Erg (my favorite)

Midline Support

If our midline or core is stable, our upper and lower body can have the right foundation of support to prevent injury. Our upper and lower back, knees, and ankles can all be supported by a stable midline, which frees up the muscles surrounding our hips to help carry that huge pack of moose meat. Proper midline support is necessary for many hunting and daily life scenarios to undertake physical activity without suffering an injury. All the movements in each of the six groups I've listed can, in various ways, strengthen our midline support by enhancing our stability and control. Nevertheless, some movements are better suited for targeting our midline as well.

Examples of movements to improve midline support:

- Front/Side Planks
- Hollow-Body Hold
- Around-the-Worlds
- Single-Arm Farmer's Carry
- L-Sit/L-Hang
- Glute Ham Developer Machine

Leg Strength

Our legs can either help us or hinder us, whether we are climbing into a tree stand, trekking for miles while carrying a heavy pack across terrain that is steep and elevated, or pursuing wild game. Strong legs reduce the risk of injuries during hunting and in daily life by stabilizing the surrounding ligaments and joints. Low back and knee problems are among the most frequent conditions people may encounter when leg strength is neglected, especially as they get older. By adding bodyweight exercises and resistance, we can build a solid foundation for leg strength that will increase our independence for a longer period of time. Legs are a crucial part of our structural basis; therefore, let's make sure we strengthen them to reduce the possibility that they slow us down. For top-notch training equipment to strengthen our legs, check out Sorinex Outdoors.

Examples of movements to improve leg strength:

- Squats
- Lunges
- Glute Bridge Holds
- Sled Pull/Push
- Split Squats
- Nordic Hamstring Curls

Rotator Cuff Stability

During our hunt, our shoulders take center stage, whether we are holding a rifle, setting up a tent, drawing a bow, or moving brush above our heads. Having a stable rotator cuff is important for keeping healthy shoulders. The rotator cuff consists of four muscles surrounding our shoulder blades (scapula). They work together to stabilize our shoulder joints and allow us to move without suffering injuries. Our shoulders can often become stiff and restricted during life. The causes of many of these painful shoulder limitations include poor postural alignment, repetitive movements, muscle imbalances, unintentional injury, under-training, and overloading with too much resistance. Improving rotator cuff stability puts our shoulders in a better position to handle both daily activities and the strenuous activity of a hunting trip.

Examples of movements to improve rotator cuff stability:

- Resistance Band Rotations
- Inverted Rows
- Snow Angels
- Plate Retractors
- Cable Pulls
- Reverse Flys

You'll notice that none of the movements listed in the categories have suggested sets or repetitions. Everyone's level of fitness varies to some extent, so it would be ideal to contact a training specialist online or at a local gym for advice on how to select the right number of total repetitions for your particular needs and goals.

There are many things to consider and explore when you reflect on your own training journey, regardless of how you immerse yourself in training, whether it be by walking a mile every morning before work, going to the gym, signing up for a workout program to do at home, or incorporating specific movements tailored for the demands of hunting. Here are some to think about:

1. It's essential to practice movements with proper technique if we want to develop fewer injuries. Good technique will help us lay a solid foundation, become fitter, and improve our health. Use online videos to learn the appropriate technique, and think about having a training specialist observe you.
2. To be able to look back on previous workouts and track your progress, get a notepad, use your phone, or download a specialized app to record the details of your training session. Record the duration, the number of reps, sets, distance traveled, and resistance utilized for a particular workout. Then, test the same workout again later. It feels good to keep ourselves accountable and measure our progress over time.
3. Consider including other movement patterns that work your muscles in different ways, such as eccentric, concentric, and isometric contractions, as they can help us build

stronger muscles, provide more stability for our joints, and help us recover from injuries.

4. One of the main causes of feeling or getting weaker as one gets older is a lack of resistance training. Using your muscles to resist a force is what is meant when something is called "resistance training." Things like lifting weights and hiking while carrying a heavy pack. If you want to get stronger, feel less weak, and have fewer physical limitations as you age, start resistance training as soon as possible. Simply get some bands, dumbbells, or kettlebells to get started, then look for online workout programs you can do with them. You'll see that seventy-five years of age is the new sixty-five, sixty-five is the new fifty-five, forty-five is the new thirty-five, and thirty-five is the new twenty-five as you start resistance training and get stronger.

5. Whether you are working out alone or with friends, turn off the music to make it more of a mental challenge. No background music pushes us to exert ourselves internally without any outside help, especially during a tough training session. I use this approach regularly in my garage by myself to elevate my mental fortitude and to shed weakness.

6. Turn up the heat. If you want to push yourself during your workouts, think about wearing long socks, sweatpants, a sweater, and a beanie (bonus points for wearing a weighted vest) to create a bigger sweat and make you uncomfortable —similar to a wrestler. I like using this approach for my aerobic capacity sessions as it makes it feel like I am breathing through a tiny straw. Of course, always make

sure you're properly hydrated before and after with water and electrolytes. Training in warm temperatures can also help mimic and better prepare us for a hunt that involves hotter weather.

Me, proudly displaying my successful hunt for a quail with my infamous bowl cut.

Growing older and observing my family hunt throughout the years sparked my interest in quail and grouse hunting. The property I grew up on was usually surrounded by wild game and birds, which was very alluring for a youngster in the fourth grade. One time we were traveling along logging roads when we spooked a covey of quail. My father pulled the vehicle over to the side of the road and told me to "jump out quick" as he applied the brakes. I recall rushing out of the truck with my 410 in hand, both anxious and excited.

My fitness level allowed me to be swift, quick, and speedy in these situations. Looking back, these were the first times my father tested my independence in the woods by leaving me alone. He also helped me to comprehend the relationship between harvesting wild game and subsequently consuming it. My mind started to become aware of what I was doing, and I was beginning to develop a viewpoint on hunting and how it was benefiting me in multiple ways.

BIOMECHANICS

The science behind the mechanics and movement of the human body is known as biomechanics. It focuses on how our bones, muscles, tendons, and ligaments interact with our movement patterns. To understand how muscular imbalances and bad posture can cause injuries and joint discomfort, as well as how to prevent and treat them, biomechanics becomes extremely crucial.

Although physiotherapists are educated to identify particular movement patterns, postures, and muscular imbalances, anyone can learn to be more aware of their own risk factors for injuries. Biomechanics was actually one of my students' favorite topics when I taught anatomy and physiology at a local high school because it is a subject that they can utilize in their daily lives.

Knowing certain movement patterns and how they affect our bodies as we age can help us fix and neutralize them when they're appropriately addressed. The following examples of improper mechanics should be recognized: duck feet, valgus knee, lumbar lordosis, and kyphosis.

Duck Feet

When you are sitting or standing, look at your feet. Do your feet face forward in a straight line, or do they slant slightly outward?

Duck feet may be the cause if that's the case. You will likely start to notice this typical postural dysfunction if you start observing other people's foot placement as they stand, sit, or even stroll.

Our feet can spin outward for various reasons, including genetics, but it is more commonly cultivated over time by lifestyle habits, tight muscles, and bad posture. When the foundation (our feet) of our body changes, a chain reaction travels up to our knees, hips, and back to try and balance the compensation below. This can create a domino effect of pain and injuries that stem from the foundation of our body—our feet.

By consciously concentrating on sitting, standing, and walking with our feet facing forward, we can easily implement a simple method to assist in correcting duck feet. Retraining our mind and body can assist in restoring the neutral position of our lower half. Various hip and lower limb muscles can also be stretched and strengthened to aid with specific needs and to address this imbalance. To find out which precise muscles to stretch and strengthen to make sure the feet start pointing forward and reduce limitations in the future, think about getting in touch with a training specialist or physiotherapist, or watch educational videos.

Another typical instance of duck feet that several clients have brought to my attention involves one foot shifting outward while the other remains forward. This posture frequently involves leaning to one side when standing or even sitting. Standing, for instance, with our feet facing forward takes more work than leaning to one side of our body, which is why we frequently unconsciously do it. But easier doesn't always equate to better. As a result, one hip may have to support greater weight than the other. When leaning to one side while standing or sitting becomes a long-term habit, it can cause low back pain, muscular imbalances, hip dysfunction, and higher chances of requiring hip surgery in the future. By holding their child on one side of their body, many parents who are carrying children experience this typical position.

When you go hiking or hunting, consider this. Do you notice yourself leaning to one side of your body to relax when you stop walking? Imagine spending years in that position. Now that you've seen an example of compensation like this, you can see why one side of our body could start to display physical pain, discomfort, or injury.

Valgus Knee

Our knees appear to pitch inward when we have valgus knees, often known as knock knees. In this position, joints are put under additional stress, which increases the risk of injuries like the medial collateral ligament (MCL) and meniscus tears of the knee. The inner area of our knees may ache when hiking up and down hills for various reasons, including any degree of valgus knees.

It is possible to treat the majority of valgus knees if they are lifestyle based, which is good news. To help our knees and feet become more aligned with fewer restrictions, we can stretch and strengthen specific muscles around our hips, groin, and legs with the help of a training specialist. To avoid injuries, deliberately concentrate on sitting, standing, and walking with your feet and knees pointed forward. Check out Ben Patrick's work for further details on how to enhance knee health (The Kneesovertoesguy).

Lumbar Lordosis

When our hips are pushed back, and our chest/belly are pushed forward, we are in an overextended position, which causes lumbar lordosis. When this happens, our lumbar spine can become overly compressed, leading to chronic low back tightness. There are a few ways we can correct this postural imbalance.

The first strategy is to squeeze your glutes continuously for seven days while walking or standing. If you forget during one of those days, you start over. Your pelvis begins to realign into a better posture (more neutral) when you squeeze your glutes (tuck your hips in), allowing the muscles around your hips to stabilize your lower back. The weight of your spine is then supported by your hips more effectively as your lower back is relieved of some of the tension.

The second strategy is to take a more methodical approach by strengthening the glutes and midline (core) region while stretching the hip flexor muscles. Regularly employing this method, slowly but surely, enables our body to realign our pelvis, relieving pressure on our spine from the lower back. A front plank, when performed correctly, is an excellent movement to use to improve posture and reduce lumbar lordosis. This was previously discussed in the midline support section.

Kyphosis

Often known as texting neck, kyphosis is the term used for the upper spine's rounding or hunching. When we unconsciously push our head forward and downward due to lifestyle variables and habits, it frequently manifests into poor posture. As technology use, specifically the computer and phones rise over time, this condition eventually impacts younger and older generations.

Our neck and upper back muscles support our head when it is balanced over our spine in a neutral position. When our head is pushed forward, most of its weight is concentrated on our cervical spine, which can become so stressed that our body is forced to begin subconsciously building extra muscle in the back of the neck to bring our neck back into alignment.

Imagine that we are in a kyphosis-like position, wearing a large pack and launching arrows frequently. In this situation, we might be fostering a future injury and developing further compensation patterns all across our bodies. Since our alignment and posture are compromised, this position may inevitably lead to shoulder pain when shooting our bow and even prevent us from hunting.

A posture check or imaging, such as an X-ray, can be used to distinguish kyphosis. Stretching and strengthening the muscles in our upper back, chest, neck, and chin is the quickest and least invasive way to help correct kyphosis if we have any degree of it. Additionally, it can be beneficial to deliberately lift our sternum and chest upward until we feel our shoulder blades merge. This enables our shoulders to return to a more effective position, which in turn aids in realigning the head and neck. Depending on the severity, we can gradually improve our posture by being consistent over time. We will experience improved breathing, decreased headaches and neck tension, and increased shoulder range of motion once we correct this postural position. Due to a properly aligned spine and improved blood supply to the brain, simply having better posture can boost mental wellness.

Last Straw Theory

The last straw theory is one of the areas of biomechanics that merits discussion. As you reach down to grab your hunting pack—which isn't usually heavy for you—you end up straining a muscle on the side of your lower back. According to the last straw theory, reaching for the pack may not have actually caused the injury.

For instance, the continuous tension and overuse from the past few months of continuously shoveling dirt in our backyard from one side of our body may have caused the injury. Future injuries, such as muscular strains and tears, can develop from repetitive movements that are not balanced across the body. Reaching down to pick up a hunting pack that is not very heavy for us is an example of how these movement deficiencies and imbalances may not appear right away but may appear when we least expect them. The last straw for our back was reaching down to pick up that hunting pack.

The significance of this theory is in being conscious of one's own tendency to repeat particular movement patterns. If a physical injury occurs at some point in our life, automatically pointing the finger directly at the movement we were doing at that moment may not be the answer. However, with injuries and imbalances, this is not always the case. Sometimes the source of our discomfort is a single movement error. Consider your daily movement patterns, which could have contributed to a deficiency and served as the last straw for that injury. Be more self-aware of them.

This last straw theory is also deeply connected to the notion that just because our bicep muscle hurts doesn't mean the bicep is the issue. We could have a tight muscle near the bicep or even on the opposite side of the body, making the bicep pull and express discomfort.

For instance, I had a client who had been experiencing right-side knee pain since completing a half-marathon six months earlier. It turns out that their left calf and ankle were extremely tight from earlier housekeeping, which forced the entire right side of the body to compensate and put extra strain on the right knee when jogging. This is an excellent example of the fact that just because we have a muscle group that occasionally feels uncomfortable, it doesn't indicate that group is always the problem. It's possible that the source of our discomfort is coming from the same side of our body or on the opposite side.

It's crucial to realize that muscles are interconnected and act both together and in opposition to one another. As a result, when one or more are overworked and compromised, another may pull tight to keep us functioning or produce pain. Our outer hip muscles, such as our glutes, assist in pulling our knee outward while the muscles on the inner part of our thighs pull it inward. This tug of war between the muscles keeps us moving and warns us when we become unbalanced through the discomfort. This does not necessarily imply that our left quadriceps always cause our right ankle problems. We must repeatedly test specific stretches and ranges of motion to find the source of the imbalance and be aware that every person has a unique situation that is distinct from others.

In this picture from the '90s, my father is holding up the longbow overhead with my brother (bottom center right), his friends, and me (far left).

The camp shown in the photo above is where I experienced many of my favorite memories. At this point, my father started instructing me on how to feel more at ease walking at night in the woods without a flashlight. When we first started walking at night in the woods, I was a nervous wreck. But with time, perseverance, and the appropriate mentoring, my father was able to help me rewire my brain so that I could adapt and develop a better relationship with the dark. Now that I think about it, going for a nighttime walk in the woods can provide us a chance to work on our biomechanics because we'll become more aware of our movement patterns. Each step is taken with complete awareness, control, and clarity.

STATIC STRETCHING

Simple static stretching is one of the most underutilized health-promoting strategies. Static stretching, in my opinion, becomes more crucial as we age. Static stretching is maintaining specific positions for a specified period of time in order to increase the range of motion and reduce stiffness. Static stretching helps with blood flow improvement, decreasing muscle and tendon stiffness, and improving flexibility. It can also help with reducing stress and headaches. All of those benefits appear to be good for our health, but the problem is that we frequently believe we don't need to stretch since we think we feel fine. I thought I could just avoid stretching while I was a college student. The ironic part is that in retrospect, I could have avoided the majority of the seven different muscle strains I experienced by routinely stretching.

Now, having decided that seven strains were a sufficient quantity, I consistently strive to complete at least ten minutes of static stretching every day using a variety of movements. I usually begin with my ankles (which serve as our basis) and slowly stretch the muscles of my legs and hips before moving up into my shoulders and arms. Depending on how I feel after training each week, I change up the stretches. Since I started doing this, I've not only become more limber and improved my flexibility when performing daily tasks, but I also feel more equipped physically to take on challenges during my training sessions and backcountry hunts.

Stretching can make us less prone to injury and ensure that we have the physical capabilities to continue hunting. Try stretching your legs and hips while at camp or during a pause in the hunt to avoid lower back tightness—especially if you frequently have a big pack on. You can benefit greatly from using things like logs, rocks, and trees to leverage a nice stretch. Get into a lunge position, for instance, during camp. Put your back foot up on something or up against something, like a tree, with the bottom of your shoe facing the sky and your laces facing downward. Having raised the back foot, slowly begin to lift your chest until you feel a stretch at the front of your hip of the leg behind you. Then, while you push forward with the leg that is behind you, be sure to squeeze your glute muscle as well. Stretch while squeezing and press for ten seconds, then relax for twenty seconds. Depending on your preference, hold this stretch for one to two minutes. Move the knee that is on the ground toward the tree that your foot is leaning against to make it more intense. Your hips will be in a position that can provide more leverage and a deeper stretch of the hip flexors as a result—a prime example of how a stretch like this can relieve some lower back tightness while you're out hunting and keep your body prepared for the demands of the hunt.

Use online tools, apps, books, and your neighborhood physical therapists to receive suggestions on various stretches that suit your needs and goals. Make it a point to try to fit in at least ten minutes of static stretching each day throughout the off-season. Your body, mind, and potential hunts will all benefit.

MOBILITY

The ability to control movement through a range of motion is referred to as mobility. You might think that mobility and static stretching are the same things, but they are actually different. Static stretching just focuses on flexibility, whereas mobility combines flexibility and stability. Both are crucial. Mobility is also a concept that enables us to handle movement-related issues like muscular tightness and pain with planned solutions. By using the proper muscles that are required to avoid injury, adopting mobility techniques allows us to be in a favorable position to hoist that heavy bison hind quarter to place on top of a tailgate.

The use of a foam roller to reduce muscular tightness and soreness and increase range of motion is a typical mobility technique that many find to be effective. Roll out your leg and hip muscles, for instance, for fifteen minutes. After that, perform five slow, controlled squats to strengthen your stability in your new, increased range of motion.

Mobility can help us achieve this goal and is simple enough to implement whether we're just starting to train or have been training for years. If we plan to hunt for a long time and want to learn how to take care of our muscular aches and pains and range-of-motion restrictions, mobility can help us. For your particular needs, take into consideration researching online mobility resources.

This picture brings back great memories of hunting early-season archery on the coast in Oregon with my mother and father.

Try hunting with a recurve or longbow if you want to be profoundly humbled. Hunting with either makes you appreciate both current technology and how hunting was in its beginnings. I have been surrounded throughout my life by people who have used traditional bows for a long time. One of them was Gary Sentman, who held the world record for the heaviest traditional bow pulled at 176 pounds in the 1970s. Every hunting season, my dad and I would travel to Gary's residence in Eastern Oregon to check out some of the new bows (as shown in the photo) that Gary was creating for his company, Moosejaw Longbows.

Whether we're pulling back a 176-pound traditional bow or simply a modernized compound bow, we may occasionally experience shoulder restrictions. Static stretching and mobility routines could be advantageous to use daily if this is the case. Wouldn't it be lovely to draw our bow back without experiencing any pain or discomfort?

ATHLETIC INJURY RECOVERY

Imagine we get a physical injury months before our annual hunt. There are several ways we might handle the situation to position ourselves to recover better in time for that hunt, depending on the severity and type of injury.

RICE is a phrase you may be familiar with. RICE stands for Rest, Ice, Compression, and Elevation, and it was developed as a model for treating injuries sustained in sports of all types. For quite some time, this protocol has been recommended as the way to recover from an athletic injury. Now, there might be a different angle worth looking into that suggests full rest, and the application of ice to athletic injuries could delay the healing process.[6]

Imagine we are hunting argali in Mongolia. Cliffs, high mountains, and difficult terrain. On one of the days, as we descend a hill, we trip over a rock and severely twist one of our ankles. It's bad enough that it instantly becomes purple and black and swells to a degree we've never known. Okay, so let's talk about the injury process now that we have an injury in mind.

Like when we have an infection, our body sends signals to start the healing process when tissue damage occurs. These signals are sent to deploy our immune system's repair squad (stem cells, macrophages), who then rush to the injured area and produce the hormone insulin-like growth factor (IGF-1), which aids in the healing process of the tissue.

However, by preventing the body from releasing IGF-1, icing an athletic injury may actually be slowing down the healing process.

When we apply ice, the blood vessels in and around the injured area constrict, closing off oxygen and blood flow. The healing immune cells (stem cells and macrophages) cannot reach the injured area to begin healing when blood flow and oxygen are cut off. Parts of the injured location's tissue may even die due to decreased blood flow brought on by icing (which traps the waste in) and may result in permanent nerve damage and other physical problems.[7]

How we can make sure that our body can successfully complete this healing process is the crucial question to ask. Applying heat and engaging/massaging muscles (using specific movement patterns) close to and around the injured area to increase blood flow can help move waste (swelling) through the body and restore circulation. Consequently, the injured area may be able to heal and recover more quickly.

But why do some claim that following an athletic injury, ice feels better? This might be because icing blocks pain receptors. But that doesn't necessarily mean that healing is occurring. When trying to block the pain after an athletic injury, icing may be beneficial. Depending on the individual, situation, and injury, a course of action can vary. Consider the ankle that was injured while hunting argali. Likely, you won't have a heating pad handy to use on the injury. Additionally, you applied for this hunt for twenty-five years, and you still have six days left. Ask yourself, "What do I need to do in this situation to ensure that I can, at least, to some degree, continue hunting?" Maybe you take NSAIDs and soak your ankle in a local creek to relieve the agonizing pain because it is that bad. And since your swelled ankle is so big, you trim the side of your boot so it can fit more comfortably inside of it. But you want your boot to feel snug and secure, so you also duct tape it to ensure it stays compact.

In a case like this, do whatever it takes to allow you to resume your pursuit of a once-in-a-lifetime hunt.

If the rolled ankle had happened months before the hunt and your main concern was to create an environment inside of your body that would allow it to recover efficiently, then applying heat and gently engaging and massaging the muscles around the area might be something to think about. Especially if you can endure the discomfort. I've utilized this method for various injuries, including a meniscus tear, along with grounding sessions (more on this later) and was able to speed up the healing process and restore my range of motion. Now bear that in mind. For my particular injury and circumstance, this strategy was effective. Each person reacts differently to injuries, and numerous injuries could happen that require various medical treatments. Reaching out to a qualified professional for your unique needs ultimately matters.

At the very least, though, now you have a better idea of the healing process for athletic injuries. According to what I've learned, boosting blood flow by applying heat and engaging/massaging the muscles close to the injured area appears useful in many cases for accelerating recovery. If your goal is to block the feeling of pain and discomfort, icing also appears to be fairly effective. The right course of action for your particular needs will depend on your goals in relation to the injury.

Ways #17–22 to Age Better and Prevent Disease

17. Establish your purpose-driven reason for consistent training.
18. Improve your foot speed, grip strength, aerobic capacity, midline support, leg strength, and rotator cuff stability through different movements.
19. Improve your biomechanics and posture to minimize injuries and range-of-motion restrictions.
20. Static stretch to some degree every day.
21. Incorporate mobility practices for injury prevention.
22. Use heat and movement (specific to the athletic injury) to increase blood flow and assist with recovery. Use ice to block unmanageable pain.

CHAPTER 3

FOCUS ON THE LONG TERM

Dietary Habits as a Way of Life

Dietary habits is a subject that is constantly evolving, particularly in regard to the foods and liquids that we should and should not consume. It's common to feel overwhelmed or confused about where to start and what may work best for a particular person when we consider the vast array of ideas, documentaries, and advertisements. The majority of individuals agree that improving our dietary habits is crucial for achieving better physical, mental, and spiritual health. There are many dietary recommendations available; my goal is to provide those that seem realistic, manageable, and tailored to achieve long-term outcomes and health.

My philosophy on long-term dietary habits can be summed up in two words: *balance* and *variety*. Avoid being overly strict and indulging in too many treats, while also trying many different foods. Although they sound simple when you first hear them, many of us find it difficult to adopt them for some reason genuinely. Luckily, I was fortunate to meet with a centenarian who could provide evidence of how nicely *balance* and *variety* worked. Dolly was her name, and she was a remarkable woman. A 102-year-old close family friend at the time. She lived a life of high quality. She even out-danced me for an hour straight at her ninetieth birthday party. It got to the point where I was so worn out that she had to start looking for a better date for the dance floor who could handle her energy and moves.

We had a lot of wonderful conversations about life, happiness, and, of course, habits that may have helped her live a long life. I once asked her what she thought about people's dietary habits as one of my questions. To my surprise, it wasn't because she followed a strict diet or thought a particular food was the best or worse. She valued *balance* and *variety*. Consuming things that grow from the earth or move on it, and enjoying the occasional glass of wine, dark chocolate, or pie. For instance, at a friend's house, she enjoyed herself while indulging in crackers and cheese. Then, when she returned home, she ate a diversity of foods that she had grown herself, like fruits, vegetables, and fermented foods, along with wild-caught fish and wild game. *Balance* and *variety* is a simple way to live life and maintain health.

The last thing she wanted to do was adhere to a rigid diet plan that was so restrictive that it caused her to develop a negative relationship with food and resulted in binge eating, stress eating, or cravings. This worked really well for her. A small quantity of nourishing foods and a small quantity of treats of various kinds. Sounds doable and reasonable, right?

It's ironic looking back that she didn't even credit her dietary habits or the fact that she exercised regularly, spent time in nature every day, lived close to her family and friends, and tended to her garden as major factors in her longevity and high quality of life, even though they all undoubtedly contributed. Dolly emphasized frequently the value of adopting an optimistic attitude, particularly while dealing with the bad outcomes that can happen in our life. For a happy and healthy life, she advised me to "live," "laugh," and "love." Take note of the connections between each of these traits and the concepts mentioned in Chapter 1 and throughout the book.

In the end, well-rounded dietary habits help us experience more opening days and hunting opportunities, as well as having a better quality of life and better health. We can live our lives with *balance* and *variety* if we want; it's quite simple. To start, let's first look at the foods that grow from the earth and the ones that move on it. These are called nourishing foods.

NOURISHING FOODS

In this context, "nourishing" refers to whole foods from a good quality source, which are required for healthy development and survival, and have a positive impact on our genes. These foods could include meat, fish, vegetables, and fruit. If you can imagine eating the majority of these kinds of foods, they most likely contain sufficient amounts of vitamins, minerals, proteins, carbs, and fats for optimal health. Finding out which of these foods makes us feel good and which ones don't is important while consuming them. This is where *variety* comes in.

Consider your family's diet when you were a child for a moment. What types of foods were provided? Was there anything that wasn't? Several factors have contributed to how our families and ancestors have eaten throughout the years. Different regions of the world have access to varying types of foods. Our genetic makeup has evolved over time to process and adapt to what our environment has to offer at any given time. This is equally true for the types of food we ate as children and the kinds of food we eat now. What we eat impacts how our body and mind currently function, whether for the better or worse, and how our genes are expressed and passed on to future generations.

Each generation consumes a variety of foods, which affects how people react well to some and less favorably to others. For example, some vegetables may digest well for you but not for me; others may require more protein or more carbohydrates. Consuming particular foods over time causes individual variances. It is crucial to realize that everything we ingest has some effect on our body, mind, and DNA.

> Think about the relationship between the food we put out for wild game like deer. The foods a deer eats may have an influence on its DNA, and when we eat the meat, the same things could have an impact on our health.

This explains why different people react differently to the same foods, leading to things like food sensitivities, joint discomfort, foggy thinking, bloating, weight gain, and stomach problems. Even different methods of cooking foods like pan frying, boiling, steaming, grilling, and baking or eating raw foods can also change how we respond to certain foods.

It might be challenging for everyone to find the right foods to fuel and nourish their bodies. Because of this, it's quite unlikely that one "diet" will become the perfect solution for everyone. Access, heredity, current health, age, personal goals, body composition, and exercise levels are just a few of the variables that affect this. Doesn't that sound like a challenging mathematical algorithm?

Here is a simple explanation of what I mean. Each person must determine what foods are best for them to eat. However, it is possible to begin with nourishing foods that are generally thought to be easier to digest that many respond well to. The trick is realizing that this might change depending on where you are in the world.

You may have access to other foods besides those I describe that are found in the United States if you reside in Australia, Alaska, Canada, or Europe, for example. If this is the case, you must do a thorough investigation to determine which foods are more nourishing in your region and which ones are less so. You probably already know what your body can digest well or what tends to give you a bubble gut at home or while you're out hunting (we've all experienced it).

Simply incorporating new foods into our diet during the off-season allows us to see how our body reacts both physically and mentally. Here is a list of my favorite nourishing foods with which you might experiment:

Meat & Fish	Fruits	Vegetables	Miscellaneous
Anchovies	Apple	Artichokes	Aged Cheese
Beef	Apricots	Asparagus	Apple Cider Vinegar
Bison	Avocado	Beets	Beef Tallow
Chicken	Banana	Bok Choy	Bone Marrow
Clams	Blackberries	Broccoli	Butter
Crab	Blueberries	Brussels Sprouts	Coconut Oil
Goat	Cantaloupe	Cabbage	Dark Chocolate
Herring	Cherries	Carrots	Eggs
Lamb	Cranberries	Celery	Ghee
Lingcod	Dates	Collard Greens	Homemade Sourdough Bread
Lobster	Kiwi	Cucumber	Honey
Oysters	Lemon	Garlic	Maple Syrup
Pork	Mango	Kale	Oatmeal
Rockfish	Oranges	Mushrooms	Olive Oil
Salmon	Papaya	Potato	Organs
Sardines	Peach	Red Cabbage	Psyllium Husks
Shrimp	Pear	Spinach	Rice
Smelt	Plum	Sweet Potato	Sauerkraut
Trout	Raspberries	Swiss Chard	Sour Cream
Tuna	Red Grapefruit	Tomato	Walnuts
Turkey	Strawberries	Yam	Wild Game Fat
Wild Game	Watermelon	Zucchini	Yogurt

Specifics to strive for, which I highly recommend:	
Local grass-fed meat and dairy products	Unrefined and extra-virgin cooking oils
Wild-caught fish	Locally sourced fruits and vegetables
Pasture-raised eggs	Raw honey

The next step is to determine the amount of each food needed once you've experimented to see what types of nourishing foods you respond well to. More specifically, the appropriate amount of each food group for you. For instance, I've discovered that when I follow the dietary ratio levels below for each meal, I feel and function the best. I strive to have roughly 50 percent of my plate made up of some combination of proteins (wild game, grass-fed meat, or wild-caught fish), 25 percent of it made up of fruit, and 25 percent of it made up of vegetables. Remember that while this works for me, it might not be the best option for you.

A helpful starting point for determining your ratios per meal (amount) is to start experimenting with the grams of protein to consume. Experiment with consuming .5–1.0 grams of protein per pound of body weight per day from meat or fish. If you weigh 200 pounds, for instance, you will eat 100 to 200 grams of protein daily, divided by the number of meals you would have. This is a good starting point that can change for what meets your own needs depending on activity levels, age, body composition, goals, etc.

Focusing on our protein needs could be effective in assisting us in achieving the body we desire by reducing body fat and maintaining muscle. Maintaining muscle gets more difficult as we age. Protein from meat or fish is muscle. So, in a way, visualize eating more muscle foods (meat and fish) to keep muscle. Off course, resistance training helps maintain muscle as well, so don't forget about that!

Consuming more protein from meat or fish may also help reduce cravings, make us feel more full (resulting in less snacking), increase our intake of vitamins and minerals that are easier to digest, keep energy consistent, and are lower in calories. Reread that last benefit if you want to lose weight and maintain it. Then, reread it again.

When I mention meat, I don't mean lunchmeat or processed meat like hotdogs; rather, I mean whole-food meat like steaks and ground burgers. The processing and additional ingredients in protein shakes and bars, which may create digestive issues like bubble gut or frequent gas, mean that they do not count as protein sources in this context. It matters what kind of protein we consume.

From what I have seen, it can be difficult to lose weight and reduce body fat since, typically, the less protein we consume from meat or fish, the more likely we are to consume higher amounts of carbohydrates, usually in the form of packaged foods. Monitoring our protein intake by calculating grams can help us determine how much to eat at each meal (portion awareness) and potentially prevent additional weight gain. In time, with practice, it becomes more possible for us to be able to identify the proper quantity and portion of protein without having to calculate grams.

Choose a few fruits and vegetables for the remainder of your plate based on the amount that makes you feel satisfied after calculating your protein intake for your particular needs. You might be wondering about the "Miscellaneous" section. These additional foods have a positive effect on both my body and mind; therefore, I periodically include them in my weekly eating regimen. Do your own experiments to see what works best for you, keeping in mind that while these foods are good for me and my body, they may not be as good for your particular needs.

Once we've determined which foods, amounts, and portion sizes are best for us, we can get creative with our meal combinations. Here is an example of some nourishing meals you can create if you need some ideas. We'll use the example of three meals a day as it's common.

Meal 1: Small bowl of yogurt with blueberries and honey, half-pound venison burger with three eggs and avocado.

Meal 2: Steamed broccoli, rice, ten-ounce elk steak with butter and unrefined salt, and an apple.

Meal 3: Baked sweet potato with sour cream, barbequed asparagus, eight-ounce salmon fillet, and dark chocolate.

The idea is to consume a portion (quantity) that makes us feel content. Eating till we have a slight sense of fullness is another way to think of eating until we are content. If we don't want to count calories, this is a terrific strategy because our body will let us know when it gets the right quantity, if we listen. Another way to make sure we eat the appropriate amount of food is to chew our food thoroughly and for a longer period of time. We may be able to get closer to eating the required quantity of food for our individual needs using this approach.

We already possess the ability to control our portions; we simply need to practice. Overeating, eating too quickly, and stuffing oneself with food can all result in bad eating habits and long-term health implications. Therefore, developing the qualities of control and patience as well as self-awareness of the portion of food that works for our particular needs may take practice, but it is extremely important. Our ability to follow these dietary strategies will improve the more consistent we are.

Because it is straightforward and getting easier every day, I have sustained this eating style for the past six years. My thinking abilities, energy, mental well-being, physical health, and sleep have all improved due to experimenting with the types and quantities of foods that make up my regular meal. All elements that can be attainable for any hunter.

Prevention Mindset: Invest Now, Save Later

Most people would agree that buying nourishing foods at the grocery store can be more expensive. It can often be difficult to rationalize spending money on nourishing food, especially if you have a limited budget or are a saver. However, the expense is worth it in the long run as an investment in your health. Personally, I like to believe that by investing in nourishing foods now, I may perhaps be able to avoid or reduce future medical expenses, clinic visits, or hospital costs associated with certain health limitations. Of course, some things are difficult to prevent, but at the absolute least, I am attempting to ensure I have the greatest possible health outcomes. It's worth the investment now to save ourselves later when we consider the costs of years of prescription medication, medical bills, and poor quality of life due to our health.

Consider spending less money on items like alcohol, dining out, a new phone, clothes, and TV subscriptions. This sacrifice will benefit you both now and in the future. Your body and mind will appreciate you spending a bit more money on higher-quality foods if you have a strategy in place. Notice how I didn't mention hunting gear...

What if we have a busy schedule with work, family, and other obligations that make it difficult for us to make time to cook even though we can afford these foods? No matter how busy we are, there is a wonderful way around this obstacle. It's called meal prepping. Cooking and preparing our meals ahead of time for the following week ensures we can consume nourishing foods.

Here is an example of how to begin meal prepping on Sunday for the coming week.

STEP 1: Acquire nourishing foods from hunting, fishing, your garden, and at the supermarket.

STEP 2: For this example, our protein of choice is a deer neck roast. Place it in a crockpot with carrots, potatoes, and herbs.

STEP 3: While venison and vegetables are cooking, cut up whole fruit and select a few miscellaneous foods (similar to what I listed) and place them into small glass containers for the upcoming week.

STEP 4: Once venison and vegetables are done cooking, put the desired amount for each meal into glass containers for the upcoming week.

STEP 5: Place all food containers in the fridge.

Quite simple, huh? This is an example of a meal that you could consume daily. Once you develop this habit, you can gradually begin incorporating a wide range of various foods and meals. Meal prepping is a fantastic alternative to relying solely on fast food and dining out.

It's okay to indulge in eating out, but going overboard might harm our health. Regardless of the kind of food we order from restaurants and fast-food places, unless we specifically inquire, we won't know exactly what was used to prepare it, what the ingredients are, how it was stored, how long the shelf life is, or if the kitchen has been kept clean. Regularly dining out may lead to or worsen digestive problems and physical and mental health issues. We can avoid these unknowns, save money, and significantly enhance our health by meal prepping. By planning our meals ahead of time, we can also reduce our risk of overeating and increase our access to a wider *variety* of foods and nutrients to prevent meal boredom. Instead of reverting to old habits every few weeks or months, meal prepping allows us to maintain consistency for years and decades. The less we embrace dietary habits like meal prepping, the more money we might spend on eating out, nutritional challenges, and programs. *Balance* is key. Eat out with your hunting companions and family if you want to. Be aware, though, that if you experience any digestive or mental health issues, it might be best to limit your dining out.

Our knees might not hurt as bad climbing that mountain, thanks to losing a few pounds, if we spend more money on nourishing foods and less on other things. By consuming high-quality protein, carbohydrates, and fats, we'll feel satiated for longer. Our physical health and mental clarity will significantly improve. And we'll probably be able to continue doing what we love—hunting—for longer.

An extraordinary and unforgettable day. This is the first black-tailed buck I harvested and the only one my father was a part of before his passing from lymphoma cancer the following summer before my senior year in high school.

This hunt still stands as the most memorable harvest I have experienced. Let me explain why. Have you ever had a gut feeling that you should visit a certain location at a certain time? Well, this image is a good representation of that. My father bought a GPS we hoped to use for fishing and hunting while I was a junior in high school during rifle deer season. We discovered a feature that computed wildlife feeding times based on the phases of the sun and moon. My father suggested that we look at the feeding hours the evening before the last day of deer season. According to the GPS, the ideal feeding period was from 8:00 a.m. to 10:00 a.m. He was curious as to the dependability of these feeding times. My father then explained the strategy to my buddy and me for the last day of the season that evening. The plan was to sleep in and wake up at 7:15 a.m. to search for deer in an older clear-cut down the road. By 8:00 a.m., as recommended by the feeding time, he wanted us to be at the bottom of the clear-cut.

The next morning, my buddy and I slept late, woke up at 7:15, and left our home shortly after for our final deer hunt of the year in dad's truck. When we arrived at the place, my father decided to wait in the truck and read while we took a twenty-minute hike up a rather steep hill. At around 8:00 a.m., we reached the bottom of the clear-cut. A large three-point deer in the middle of the rut approached us at 8:02 a.m., wandering out of the woods while grazing. I took that buck at ten yards at around 8:04 in the morning. Two minutes within the feeding time that was designated according to the GPS, that deer walked out. I can assure you that we might not have seen this deer if we had gotten up early as usual and arrived at the bottom of that clear-cut at first light, which was at that time 6:45 a.m. We dashed back down the hill to tell dad with joy. My father was giddy with excitement for us. We broke down the deer, transported it back to the truck, and then drove home.

This book was written in part to hopefully assist parents and/or soon-to-be parents in making better lifestyle choices so their offspring won't have to go through what I experienced. Due to his strenuous martial arts training and various labor work around our property, my father was physically active. Even if he engaged in physical activity and spent a lot of time outside, this does not guarantee perfect health free from sickness. As previously said, numerous factors contribute to one's health (lifestyle choices). My parents had recently divorced; he was under chronic stress linked to his finances; he was receiving little to no good quality sleep; and he frequently had poor dietary habits at the time. Consistently making unhealthy lifestyle choices for years, months, or even just a few weeks can add up and surprise you.

TREAT ALLOWANCE

Like any long-term habit, it's critical that things seem realistic and attainable. You all want to know about *balance* in dietary habits, so let's talk about that. I believe it's essential for us to avoid feeling fully restricted, in addition to giving our body and mind nourishing foods. The truth of the matter is that occasionally, whether at home, while traveling, while hunting, or in other situations, we may feel the want to indulge in a food or drink that is not ideal for our diet. My experiences reveal that many individuals begin a strict diet, follow it for a while, and then revert to previous habits for this reason. This does not imply that you should quit following a strict diet if you have experienced and are still experiencing positive results. I say keep going if it is working for you.

The problem is that we often keep trying new diets, fads, and fat-burning pills, signing up for yearly weight loss challenges, quick-fix detoxes, piling up on dietary supplements, and even risking surgery because we don't address the underlying root reasons why we are unable to see results. Because of our addiction to a way of thinking that works like "pushing a button" to acquire what we want, many of these approaches start to look enticing.

We usually end up back where we started or even further away from our goals when we don't address the underlying cause that keeps us from losing weight or seeing results. Many of the challenges I see people struggle with in dietary habits are not being accountable (honest with themselves) and consistent (patient enough) over an extended period of time. This results, in part, from a lack of practice and the development of new thought patterns with these traits, which subsequently translate into better dietary habits. None of these traits call for any kind of money, simply our time and effort. Being accountable and consistent can help us develop better-dietary habits that will assist us in getting the results we desire. These characteristics persist throughout time and can have a significant impact on whether we develop the physique and health we want. They are crucial for figuring out *balance* as well.

Unfortunately, eating out frequently and drinking heavily won't assist us in losing that stubborn belly fat. There is, however, a middle ground. We can occasionally eat out and have a drink while maintaining our progress toward our goals. It's called the treat allowance. For those who desire to improve their health by consuming nourishing foods while occasionally rewarding themselves to a treat, this is a realistic and manageable option. I like this strategy because it enables us to slim down, prevents binging from too much restriction, achieves our goals, and, most importantly, develops a habit that we uphold for months, years, and decades as opposed to just a few short weeks or days.

The reality of life is that having perfect dietary habits is not required to maintain robust physical, mental, and spiritual health. There is no doubt that we need to eat nourishing foods. But do we really need to be so rigid that we'll never be able to have a cinnamon roll again in our life? No, I don't think so. When we are very strict about what we can and cannot eat, we occasionally tend to develop a fear of particular foods, which can result in physiological stress reactions or even eating disorders. It's important to realize that many people indulge in occasional treats and maintain good health well into their eighties, nineties, and even after reaching one hundred. This is why I advocate for dietary habits that can be kept up for the rest of one's life, don't feel overly complicated or restrictive, improve one's health, and promote the maintenance and achievement of one's own goals. All of that entails occasionally treating ourselves, just like Dolly did.

There is no reason to feel guilty or bad about indulging in occasional treats. We are not bad people for enjoying a delicious dessert while going out with pals. It is possible to spend time with others and treat ourselves while attaining our goals and transforming into a happier, healthier version of ourselves. In the end, everything comes down to *balance*. This is true in most situations in life.

How to utilize the treat allowance. First, check to see if you are consuming the recommended amount of protein each day from meat or fish (.5–1.0 grams per pound of body weight each day). The sole requirement for enjoying a treat is this. Next, set a limit on your weekly treats so you can hold yourself accountable and give yourself some direction. You might have planned to indulge yourself in five treats throughout the course of the upcoming week, for instance. That would mean that five times a week, you grant yourself permission to eat whatever you want. A serving size that makes you feel satisfied but not overstuffed. The caveat to this approach is that if you do not see the results you want, such as a reduction in body fat, you must actively engage in self-awareness to realize that having a lower treat number may be a good bet. Additionally, if you suffer from digestion issues, high blood pressure, or high blood sugar, are less active and more sedentary, or have any other health problems, consider this advice. Because with all of these factors, you might need to cut back on fewer treats at first until you develop a routine of regularly consuming nourishing foods and making better lifestyle choices, at which point you will be where you want to be.

A lower treat number is essential for individuals with digestion problems. Our small and large intestines are home to trillions of bacteria, which play an important role in maintaining good oral hygiene, hormone balance, sleep, mental health, disease prevention, controlling a significant amount of the immune system response, and many other processes. They also aid in nutrient absorption and digestion. It would appear that gut health (starting at the mouth) has a big impact on every part of our health and greatly enhances our sense of well-being.

Poor dietary habits, such as overindulging in treats frequently and eating less nourishing foods, can weaken and damage the lining of our intestines, leaving micro-sized holes. Inflammatory responses may follow right away. These reactions frequently lead to internal turmoil and various physical and mental problems when specific hormone responses are triggered. A few of the conditions that may be partially linked to poor gut health include irritable bowel syndrome, type 2 diabetes, acne, cavities, colon cancer, heart disease, bloating, hormone imbalances, allergies, infertility, thyroid dysfunction, anxiety levels, celiac disease, memory loss, fatigue, brain fog, mood disorders, weight gain, high blood pressure, depression, and chronic gas.

There may be some truth to the Greek philosopher Hippocrates's assertion that "All disease begins in the gut." It's critical to look at the types of foods we regularly give our bodies because of the close symbiotic relationship between our gut bacteria, intestines, and overall health.

Remember that maintaining *balance* is essential. If you have digestive issues, you don't have to be perfect. Maybe consider limiting the number of treats you allow yourself, or better yet, find a healthier alternative for your specific needs that you can make yourself. There is nothing wrong with the occasional treat, but you also need to develop self-awareness to determine whether your health is getting better and whether you are moving in the right direction. Then, make any necessary modifications. When you're still receiving the desired results and having the occasional treat, you've found the treat number that works best for your needs.

One of the reasons the treat allowance seems so effective is because it allows us to indulge without going overboard in light of our needs and goals by giving ourselves a treat, like that precisely planned pizza, for example. The treat allowance is excellent for dealing with life's unexpected and planned events, such as a planned BBQ with friends, a hunting trip, a meal out with friends, a vacation, birthday parties, ice cream outings with the kids, concerts, etc. Consume nourishing foods all week and, if you'd like, save the treat for a day when something special is scheduled.

Every Sunday, write down the number of treats you're allowed to have for the coming week on your calendar and base it on an evaluation of your current health and goals. The treat allowance number you chose three weeks ago must be used, right? Absolutely not. Start by checking in with yourself to ensure your energy, physique, and mental well-being are where you want them to be. If they are not, consider eating more nourishing foods, practicing restraint, postponing satisfaction, and consuming fewer treats both during the off-season and while you are hunting. Have faith in your abilities to succeed.

Whatever number you choose for your weekly treat allowance, be as strict as you can with it and hold yourself accountable. If you fail to follow your own treat allowance for any reason (based on your goals and what you wrote) and wind up breaking it, give yourself a physical reminder, such as 150 burpees. Being honest with yourself can help you develop the self-discipline to stick to the weekly treat allowance number you recorded.

You will ultimately reach the point where you are aware of where you stand with respect to your goals and when it is suitable to treat yourself. When this occurs, you won't need to write it in your calendar because you'll know instinctively how to stay balanced so that you can indulge in a treat. Nobody else will know, only you.

Reducing the amount of treats we bring into our house is crucial when using the treat allowance. Consider making a small purchase at the grocery store to consume all at once in this situation. This might prevent us from giving in to the temptation to overeat on leftovers simply because they are at home. If an amount that equates to more than one sitting of treats somehow sneaks into your home, perform a kitchen raid.

Depending on your goals, choose a day once a month to go through the contents of your pantry, freezer, and refrigerator and eliminate everything you consider to be treats (also known as non-nourishing). Treat foods are typically packaged and processed. On the nutrition information panel of these foods, watch out for the following ingredient categories: vegetable/seed oils, refined grains/flour, processed sugars/artificial sweeteners, and soy.

Many of these ingredient categories can be found in foods like bread, cereals, crackers, chips, pasta, and other similar items. Additionally, they can be found in a few beverages, such as flavor-added coffee drinks, energy drinks, sports drinks, regular and diet sodas, and other beverages. Sadly, you may now find them in packaged foods, where you least expect to find them. Items like soups, sauces, protein bars, shakes, ready-made dinners, dressings, condiments, and spice mixes. Because a food item is advertised as having high protein levels, being organic, etc., on the front of the label, we often believe that it is healthy. However, this is not always the case if the ingredients are detrimental to our health. The lesson here is to read the ingredient label on the food products you have in your home, especially if you're trying to eat healthier on purpose. Whether you buy them or make them yourself, better options are available. An easy rule of thumb is to eat less of an ingredient if you don't know what it is or what it does to your body. Nourishing foods, including meat, fish, vegetables, and fruit, all have something in common. They each have one ingredient, themselves.

Any of these poor-quality ingredient categories consumed in excess can harm our physical and mental health in various ways. Consider vegetable and seed oils. Vegetable and seed oils sound like they should be healthy, right? Since they are comprised of plants and seeds and have been designated "heart healthy," they must be. Plus, they are listed as ingredients in a majority of food products, such as:

- Rapeseed Oil
- Soybean Oil
- Cottonseed Oil
- Sunflower Oil
- Safflower Oil
- Corn Oil
- Grapeseed Oil
- Peanut Oil
- Canola Oil

Although advertised as "heart healthy," these oils are often highly refined and turn into chemically altered, pro-inflammatory compounds at production. At the industrial level, these oils become genetically unstable due to being heated at high temperatures, put through a chemical solvent process, bleached, and deodorized into toxic products that our bodies do not recognize. When ingested frequently, this can result in unnecessary, harmful amounts of inflammation throughout our bodies, including the brain. They also devastate the lining of our intestines, which is one reason for many digestive problems that are nutritional in origin.

These oils are extremely detrimental to our health, especially when we overindulge. This explains why consuming vegetable/seed oils frequently could be connected to heart disease, autoimmune diseases, impaired memory and learning abilities, depression, anxiety, infertility, dementia, type 2 diabetes, asthma, irritable bowel syndrome, aggression, macular degeneration, and osteoarthritis.[8]

Take a break from reading this book and examine the ingredient labels on the food products you have stocked up in your kitchen if you are at home right now as you read these lines. Look for those oils; you might be surprised by what you find.

If you and your family get into the habit of routinely eating additional treats, the kitchen-raid approach is a terrific way to get everyone back on track. Recall that treats are not necessary for health or survival; rather, they are meant for momentary pleasure and to maintain *balance*.

It's critical to realize that goals are not achieved overnight. We need to have patience and trust in the process. We will make progress, such as losing weight, on certain days but not on others. Sometimes it can be discouraging and make us want to give up on our goals. Never surrender. Recall your "why" in your mind. Similar to the incentive for training that is purpose-driven. If you can keep an incentive in the back of your mind, such as "to experience more opening days and hunting opportunities," for being accountable and more consistent with your dietary habits, you'll be far more likely to stick with it. Once your dietary habits are more consistent throughout the year, you might even discover that you are less worried about putting on weight or regretting certain holiday meals. This occurs because we put ourselves into a better position before the holidays, allowing us not to feel any guilt for consuming particular foods if we so wish. How great would that be?

Maybe perhaps think about putting a reminder on your computer and phone's screen saver of your incentive (your "why") to stay consistent. Another option is to print a document with your incentive written on it, then tape it to the front of your refrigerator. You could also create a sticker to attach to your bow, or you could even get it tattooed. If you have a reminder of an incentive, such as "to experience more opening days and hunting opportunities," you'll probably continue to be driven to work toward your goals throughout the entire year.

Keep it simple, ensure you meet your daily protein requirements, fruits, and vegetables, adhere to your treat allowance, and be accountable. Try it out for yourself. Once you've found what works best for you, continue with it, especially if it enables you to remain consistent and moves you closer to your goals.

Whatever you choose to do, be open and willing to change your habits to get closer to your goals. Whatever obstacles you face, whatever slow progress seems to be going, or however discouraged you feel for whatever reason, stick with it. It all boils down to deciding if we "actually" want to accomplish our goals or only "kind of" want them. You are capable of achieving anything if you actually want it. Remember, we only get one life.

Me with a 350-pound, once-in-a-lifetime bear from the Oregon coast.

Early one October, my hunting buddy and I decided to go on a later afternoon deer hunt in a location I had never been to before. Once there, we took a thirty-minute stroll through some pristine meadows and clearings. I spotted a massive black bear standing upright twenty yards away and facing us as we walked around a huge tree. It was pure, raw adrenaline, unlike anything I'd ever felt. It's bear season, too, so I lift my rifle at once, aim, and fire. The bear is driven back by the force of my 338 before running into a narrow, steep valley. We sit down after being shaken by the adrenaline and assess what just happened. It feels like you partially black out during those moments since it happens so quickly.

The sun is setting, and it's about to get dark as we wait for thirty minutes. We walk cautiously and slowly down this ravine for about thirty yards when we hear movement in the undergrowth. We were certain that the bear was waiting for us behind a log! And I do not doubt that he didn't want to converse pleasantly. We hurried back to the truck after backing out of that spot gradually. We returned the next day to search for him because the area was cool and shaded.

The following day, we rounded up seven of our friends and took my 1998 Toyota pickup. The bear was expired behind the undergrowth we had seen the previous night. Since this was my first bear, I am not particularly good at estimating bear sizes. But based on what the local taxidermist told us, this was a huge fall black bear for the Oregon coast. It took most of us to load it into the truck's bed. Looking back, we should have snapped a photo of the vehicle because the weight nearly smashed the wheels. We used one of those spin-able disposable cameras to take this photo. It's funny how things have changed. You can tell that when we were younger, we had no idea how to arrange the bear for a good picture. Nonetheless, many happy memories are generated by this image. Dad would have been delighted for me.

As it contains high-quality protein, fats, vitamins, and minerals, properly prepared bear meat can be a terrific addition to enhancing general health. Since a bear eats a lot of plant matter, all the healthy compounds found in the plants it consumes are transferred to the meat we eat. Check out *Bear Hunting Magazine* for more details on bear hunting and its significance for conservation.

QUALITY OF FOOD WHILE HUNTING

The idea behind the foods we eat during the in-season is quite similar to the idea behind the foods we eat during the off-season, with a twist on *balance* and *variety*. The catch is that particular foods can affect how we perform when hunting. Performance includes everything like how the stalk goes, how well we aim with a bow, how tired we are as we climb the hill, how driven we are, how focused we are during a mentally taxing hunt, and so on. No matter what kind of hunting we do—in a tree stand, a blind, in the backcountry, along logging roads, etc.—the foods we eat may impact how physically and mentally we function and, to some extent, determine whether we are successful.

Consider the quality of the foods that professional athletes eat all season long. Do you think professional athletes eat well throughout the year but partake in low-quality foods when it matters the most to fuel their bodies and minds during the playoffs? This is a good example of why hunters may want to examine their nutrition before and during the hunting season.

Here's how we deconstruct this to our advantage so we can be more ready than ever for our next hunt. First, think about the kinds of food you would like to bring on your next hunt. Whatever they are, make sure to eat them during the off-season with awareness of their effects on you. Do you experience stomach pain when you consume them? Headache? Feeling worn out and sleepy? If they do, it might be a good idea to swap them out for alternatives that your body reacts to more favorably.

If you are unsure of which foods to stay away from that could impact your performance, I would generally advise consuming less packaged foods that include the previously mentioned ingredients: vegetable/seed oils, refined grains/flour, processed sugars/artificial sweeteners, and soy. Consuming foods with these ingredients frequently while hunting may negatively affect your physical and mental performance. If you wish to bring packaged food like a freeze-dried meal on your next hunt, check the ingredients to see if it contains any of these components. Assuming they do, it might be advantageous to find a better alternative if you want to reduce the risks that could compromise your performance and how you feel physically and mentally during your next hunt. Each of those ingredient categories could have a minor or substantial effect on gut health, decision-making, fatigue, sleep quality, and immune system activation, depending on the individual. Any hunt can include exceptionally high physical and mental demands; as a result, healthier alternatives could provide help and support when we most need it.

Smoked salmon, elk pepperoni, aged cheese, fruit and vegetable puree, dark chocolate, whole dried fruit, bone broth, bear sausage, walnuts, unsweetened coconut flakes, and my brother's famous homemade sweet potato pancakes are some of the higher-quality foods my hunting buddies and I bring with us into the backcountry.

Let's imagine that despite our best efforts and extensive planning, we still experience bubble guts when hunting or even during the off-season. Here is a protocol to consider the following morning that may be helpful:

STEP 1: When you wake up, drink eight ounces of water (with nothing added).

STEP 2: To help remove any extra debris from your intestines that may be causing a problem, wait until you are hungry or wait a few hours after the time you would typically eat before drinking another eight ounces of water with one to three tablespoons of psyllium whole husks (fiber) mixed in.

STEP 3: Eat whole fruit (regular or dried) until you feel a sense of fullness. This is your first intake of food.

STEP 4: Self-reflect on what could have been the cause of your bubble gut. Once you figure it out, avoid that food/liquid and eat and drink other options throughout the day.

There is no set time frame in which these steps must be completed. They simply need to be completed in that order, and for however many days it takes till you feel your stomach is back to a normal state. With its high fiber content, psyllium whole husks do a decent job of clearing out some of the food debris that may be causing you problems in your small or large intestine (colon). Fruit in its whole form is one of the easiest foods for our gut to digest and process, making it a good choice to eat after.

Whole fruit, in general, is one of the best things you can bring on any kind of hunt, in my opinion. What about the sugar in whole fruit, you might be wondering. There is a difference between the sugar contained in whole fruits like an orange and the sugar contained in packaged food and liquid items. When we eat whole fruit, our blood sugar does not spike dramatically. This enables a more balanced internal reaction with steady energy rather than the highs and lows of a processed sugar crash.

This is partly due to the other components present in whole fruits, such as water, fiber, beneficial plant compounds, and vitamins and minerals. These other components found in whole fruits balance out the sugar content for better digestion, balance, and energy. Whole fruits are easy on the digestive system, hydrate us better, give us more mental energy, boost our immune system, and balance our hormones. If you don't have access to fresh whole fruit during the off-season because of the time of year or your location, seek whole frozen fruit at the grocery store.

Elk meat staying cool on a backcountry hunting trip.

The chance to feed my family meat that is packed with nutrients is one of the most enticing aspects of hunting for me. I can't always bring food back, but when I do, we are so appreciative. In my opinion, the more self-sufficient we can become in terms of obtaining our food without the aid of others through hunting and gardening, the more money we ultimately save, the better quality food we can consume, and the more gratitude we can experience for the food given the effort involved.

Because it's still early September and it gets warm in the afternoons, a common question regarding our backcountry elk hunting trips is how to keep the meat cool. We typically build a wooden platform over a little river, as depicted in the image, and place the meat on top of it. It would be quite difficult to keep the meat cool if it weren't for the river (hence the need for self-cooling game bags). The meat doesn't only keep chilled; the wind current on top of the water also renders it odorless, reducing the likelihood that an animal will come in and feast. No matter where the sun will be, we position the meat to be shaded. We have kept meat this way for more than seven days, and the meat was well-cured and delicious.

LIQUID FOR LIFE

We have now discussed the food quality part of dietary habits; let's move on to the liquid. Also known as one of the most valuable resources on planet earth, water. Since we were young, this liquid has been recommended for us all to consume because it literally keeps us alive and healthy. Water, when consumed at sufficient and high-quality levels, enables us to function at an optimum level. Hydration, controlling body temperature, delivering nutrients and oxygen to cells, and other processes are all functions of water consumption. The key to enjoying all of these fantastic water-related advantages is to make sure we drink enough of it, taking into account our activity levels, the environment we are in, our age, and the makeup of our bodies. When talking about how much water to drink, a good place to start is to drink according to thirst or roughly half your body weight in ounces each day.

Water quality is a subject that is frequently discussed in the conservation community. Since water quality varies depending on where we are on the planet, having access to filtered water could be considered a privilege. Having filtered water would be a blessing from above for many people. When water is filtered, harmful bacteria, fluoride, plastics, pharmaceuticals, and other circulating contaminants that could have an adverse effect on human health are reduced. Less contamination is one of the reasons the mountain water we drink while hunting tastes so delicious and invigorating.

Limiting these contaminants is challenging because of population density and easy access to water. Knowing this, I urge you to seriously consider purchasing a home water filter, such as a carbon filter or a reverse osmosis system. To go one step further, add a water filter to your shower head to reduce the number of harmful contaminants that contact your skin. In the long run, both will benefit our health and well-being greatly.

Unrefined Salt

The value of unrefined salt in relation to water and hydration is one dietary topic that is frequently overlooked. Salt that hasn't been refined differs from salt that has. Refined salt is found in packaged foods like soups and frozen dinners; it is depleted of essential minerals and contains sodium that has undergone extensive processing. Most of the time, it's probably a good idea to avoid packaged foods that include refined salt. High amounts of refined salt in packaged foods are not the quality of salt we want more of; unrefined salt is.

The body requires and craves unrefined salt, such as Celtic Sea Salt®, Redmond Real Salt, and Pink Himalayan Salt. These premium salts have mineral concentrations that include electrolytes like sodium, calcium, magnesium, and potassium in their purest form. Unrefined salt is crucial for our health because it helps us stay hydrated, which is necessary for mental clarity, reduces muscle cramps, boosts energy, supports hormones, reduces sugar cravings, maintains our heart's electrical activity, improves sleep, and enhances training performance. Hunters, stay salty!

Think about hiking while carrying a large pack or ascending a mountain in Utah while pursuing Mule deer or, in the sweltering heat of Arizona, pursuing Coues deer. Electrolytes are lost through sweating and physical activity as they are needed for muscular contractions, energy production, and maintaining fluid balance throughout the body. We also use them for our thinking and focus abilities. Electrolytes from unrefined salt are essential for our body and brain to function at a high level.

It is important to consume unrefined salt with water for proper hydration. Because we can lose our electrolytes through urination, when we drink too much water and not enough unrefined salt, we can become dehydrated.

How much unrefined salt should we try to get? Depending on how much electrolytes we need and how salt-sensitive we are, it varies from person to person. Generally speaking, according to taste, sprinkle it on your nourishing foods during the off-season. Your tongue has a built-in mechanism to inform you when it has received the appropriate dosage. You might also experiment with consuming a certain amount and then check to see how your blood pressure responds. If it stays the same or improves, that amount is appropriate for you specifically. Keep in mind that if you crave salty foods, you may need to increase your intake of unrefined salt.

To enhance physical and mental performance when hunting and before and after off-season training sessions, add a pinch of unrefined salt to your water bottle and meals. For instance, since unrefined salt includes electrolytes, you can consider adding a pinch or roughly half teaspoon to your sixteen- to thirty-two-ounce water bottle to aid in the body's absorption of the liquid. If it tastes like ocean water after you've consumed it, you've added too much salt. Consider experimenting with electrolyte powders in addition to this strategy to keep you hydrated. Just make sure that the company and brand are reliable and that no unnecessary ingredients have been added.

During the off-season, in the style of a margarita, you could take a glass of filtered water and add some ice, freshly squeezed lemon juice, and lemon juice with unrefined salt to the rim. The "super hunter elixir" is the name of this hydration drink. It is so named because, you guessed it, consuming it makes you feel like a *super hunter*.

Perhaps you are already dialed in with staying hydrated on a consistent basis and are looking for some additional beverage ideas. If so, try experimenting with some of my personal favorites, such as coffee (with nothing added), tea, bone broth, and kefir.

My buddy and I with his 3x4 buck.

This image brings back some wonderful memories. My buddy and I decided to look for a black-tailed deer for him on a wet Saturday. All day, we walked through some beautiful terrain, but no bucks. One of my buddy's final excursions, which he wanted to check out and take a quick walkthrough of, was short enough for me to tell him I would sleep in the truck (probably due to staying up late and not consuming nourishing food). After closing my eyes for what felt like five minutes, my good friend returned to the truck and tells me he got a four-point! I found it hard to believe. We had not spotted any bucks that day, so it took some convincing to get me to believe it. We walked down this old, clear-cut road for approximately twenty minutes when, lo and behold, a 3x4 deer was lying on the ground. We were ecstatic. Such a wonderful memory—we dressed the deer out, hauled it back to the truck, and then drove home.

When I think back to this hunt, I realize that in addition to not regularly ingesting nourishing foods, I also did not consume any unrefined salt. Funny thing is, your energy levels seem to be more consistent throughout the day because of the electrolytes in unrefined salt. Naturally, getting a good night's sleep is also beneficial. I suppose there are times in life when the phrase "I wish I knew then what I know now" is applicable.

16:8 METHOD

As noted previously, I am a big fan of lifestyle choices that are sustainable for a long period of time. This following dietary strategy is just that and might be worth exploring once you start consistently ingesting nourishing foods. The 16:8 method is the name of it. This concept for the past five years has taken my health to the next level and beyond in terms of significant dietary changes I've made (recall the gene I have). The 16:8 method simply means fasting for sixteen hours and eating all of our food for the day in eight hours. This strategy doesn't include depriving ourselves; rather, it involves carefully planning when we eat. Ancestral DNA reveals that due to unsuccessful hunting, unfavorable weather, and constant traveling, people frequently went without food. In this instance, our body has the innate programming necessary to handle this type of fasting consistently. The following are some benefits of the 16:8 method that many people, professional athletes and myself, are experiencing:

Potential Benefits of the 16:8 Method	
Reduces body fat	Consistent energy
Better mental clarity and focus	Preserves muscle mass
Improves cardiovascular system	Enhances immune system functioning
Better quality sleep	
Improves cognitive abilities (memory/learning)	Improves blood pressure
	Saves time
Stabilizes blood sugars	Boosts aerobic capacity
Better aging	Reduces inflammation
Improves gut health	Improves training performance

An example of the 16:8 method would be having our first bite to eat at nine in the morning and finishing by five in the evening. Nutrition experts do not always agree on what can break a fast. Most of these professionals concur that water doesn't; however, others claim that drinking tea or coffee with nothing added can still allow us to experience various health benefits of a fast. In short, the moment we consume anything other than water, such as the gum we started chewing in the morning, the bacon slice, the vitamins we took, or the bagel, our fast is over, and our eating time has started.

At first, the 16:8 method can be challenging and may make us feel hungry since we are used to certain eating times. Stick with it; you will become acclimated. After a few weeks, you will get past the initial stage of hunger that is derived from your mind convincing you that you need food when you really don't yet.

A smaller period of food intake, when seen from the standpoint of health using the 16:8 method, offers our digestive system the required time to repair and recover, much like our muscles. As a result, we can consider the sixteen-hour fast as the time when our cells are being rejuvenated. After eight hours of eating, depending on the quality of the foods and liquids consumed, we can begin the process of rebuilding our bodies and cells.

It is crucial to understand that after eating, a specific amount of blood is directed from our body to our gut to assist with the process of digestion and nutrient absorption. Our immune system is unable to perform at its peak while we are fed because our body is partially focused on digestion at this time. Our immune system, body, and brain all function very well when the gut has less food (assuming we are not in a long-term starvation period).

Options

People react differently to various eating times, which is one of the most significant things I have learned and noticed while using this method. For instance, you might begin by eating for a week at a twelve-hour window, then for a week at an eleven-hour window, and so on until you reach an eight-hour window. Examine yourself and determine what time frame you feel your best physically and mentally. Due to their schedules, how they feel, and the numerous health benefits they experience, some of my clients choose to permanently adhere to a ten-hour, nine-hour, or even seven-hour time frame. Try your best to avoid consistently eating in a time frame of six hours or less so that you have sufficient time to eat enough to meet your needs, preserve muscle, and maintain hormone balance.

Starting our eating time earlier in the day would be ideal if we had complete control over our schedules because it gives us more time before bedtime to go without eating, which leads to better sleep and internal wellness (more on this later). For example, eating between the hours of 7:00 a.m. and 3:00 p.m. is better for our general health than eating between the hours of 3:00 p.m. and 11:00 p.m. Determining when your eating time begins and finishes is something to keep in mind while considering your job, family, and children and their schedule. It implies that if you and your family finish dinner by 6:00 p.m., then the time of your first meal must not be earlier than 10:00 a.m. Personally, I usually start eating around 11:00 a.m. and end by 7:00 p.m.

Once you've found your "sweet spot," stay with it and try to be as consistent as possible. Please note that you do not have to adhere to your eight-hour eating time frame for the rest of your life to reap the health benefits. For a variety of reasons, you might frequently have days when you eat outside of eight hours, and that's fine. Simply do your best to stick to the 16:8 method, given your way of life. To guarantee appropriate digestion and balance throughout the off-season, plan your meals to be consumed at or around the same time of day. For both short- and long-term health, eating at around the same times each day creates long-lasting habits essential for our well-being.

Here are a few things to consider before experimenting with the 16:8 method:

1. It is important to note that specific people such as children (younger than twelve), pregnant mothers, and breastfeeding mothers need to avoid this 16:8 method as inhibited eating when growth and hunger are sporadic, especially for a young child or fetus is not advantageous for their health.
2. If you are chronically stressed, frail, or malnourished for various reasons, it may be wise to eat within a bigger time

frame, such as nine to eleven hours, and to have your time frame start earlier in the day, such as 7:00 a.m.–4:00 p.m. to maintain proper hormone balance.

3. If you decide to incorporate the 16:8 method, consuming unrefined salt in your meals and occasionally in your water is imperative for maintaining proper electrolyte balance due to the specific timing of meals (maintaining fluid balance).
4. Do we have to eat at the same time every day while on the hunt? Absolutely not. You can try, depending on your goals and the necessary physical and mental effort, but when hunting, many factors are frequently beyond our control. Personally, I prefer to consume more food in the morning and the afternoon so that I won't be hungry when we return to camp in the late hours of the night. This method helps me get better sleep and feel refreshed when waking up due to a longer time frame of no food before bed.
5. The 16:8 method is not an excuse to consume treats (non-nourishing foods) on a regular basis. The healing and health benefits that occur while using this dietary method work best when we are consuming nourishing foods (i.e., meat, fish, vegetables, and fruit) on a consistent basis that are required for rebuilding the tissues needed for health and survival.
6. Lastly, and most importantly, if you are considering experimenting with the 16:8 method, reach out to your primary doctor (regardless of whether you are taking any medications) to make sure it is okay to start for your specific needs.

Meal Frequency

The phrase "What about meal frequency?" is commonly used in relation to the 16:8 approach. You might have heard that eating frequently will speed up your metabolism. This is a widely held idea for various reasons, but I want to present an alternative perspective. If we eat soon after our last meal, a practice known as "snacking," our gut doesn't have time to recuperate properly. If we have our first meal at 9:00 a.m. and then a snack an hour later, for example, our stomach and intestines don't get a break like they would if we waited until 1:00 p.m. to have something to eat for the second time (regardless of the amount). The constant flow of food into our intestines needs to stop for a while. Here's why.

Imagine the intestines as a school's hallway. The debris in our intestines is comparable to the occasional bit of trash left by students. Think about what would happen if the school's janitor was told only to clean the hallways while no kids were present. The janitor would have very little time to clean up if students were constantly entering and leaving trash behind. A lack of cleaning results in trash accumulation and growth. As time passes, it won't be as clean or clear as before. This is quite similar to the idea of food entering our intestines regularly through snacking. Our intestines never get a break from snacking to clear out food debris. Hence the innate process of the migrating motor complex (MMC). To make the intestines cleaner, heal, and rebuild tissues, the MMC is a series of periodic cleansing contraction waves that push food debris out of the intestines during fasting.[9] Smooth muscle lines the inside of our intestines, and they require recovery time in the same manner as our skeletal muscles. We must understand that this remarkable healing process occurs while a person is not eating. It makes sense to have some time in between meals, don't you think? Anyone who has digestive problems of any kind should consider this alternative perspective. Whatever it takes, try to put off eating for at least a few hours in between meals.

During the off-season, snacking and eating frequently may not be the best choice for long-term health. One of the reasons is to reduce the unaccounted calories we ingest when we snack, which could lead to weight gain (fat). Snack less if you want to lose more body fat. Distancing the time between meals (eating less frequently), such as eating our first meal at 9:00 a.m., second at 1:00 p.m., and last by 5:00 p.m. (eight-hour time frame), may help our intestines and gut recover, maintain stable blood sugar levels, increase fat burning, balance hormones, and improve the performance of our immune system and brain.

I believe it's crucial to consider the possible causes of our initial snacking urges followed by a plan of attack to eliminate them. Is it a result of our stress? Boredom? Procrastination? Each of these might contribute to someone's increased tendency to snack. However, inadequate sleep the night before and dietary deficiencies such as a lack of protein could also be to blame for the urge to snack. When we eat nourishing foods, especially an adequate quantity of protein each day (.5–1.0 grams per pound of body weight each day) from wild game, grass-fed meat, or wild-caught fish, it will probably be easier to space out our meals and eat fewer snacks.

I truly think that one of the primary reasons (among many others) why it is challenging to shed excess body fat is frequent snacking, especially when it involves an over-indulgence in treats. Should we refrain from snacking ever again? Of course not. Depending on your goals and situation, indulge in a snack, but watch out for overindulging. If you indulge in a snack, you might want to think about making the snack healthier by upgrading its quality. A snack like raw carrots, whole fruit, aged cheese, or liver and steak crisps (from Carnivore Aurelius).

Break*fast*

Personally, the 16:8 method has made me realize that breakfast is an important meal of the day, but in a different way than we are initially told. Breakfast, in my mind, is an important meal of the day as it's the first food we bring into our bodies after fasting. Hence the term "break-fast." This is why having a breakfast full of nourishing foods for our body allows it to refuel and rebuild—a meal such as an eight-ounce venison steak with unrefined salt, butter, a small bowl of rice, asparagus, and a banana.

In general, if we aim for our first meal of the day to have a sufficient amount of protein from wild game, grass-fed meat, or wild-caught fish, as mentioned previously, there is a good chance we can reduce body fat, maintain muscle, reduce cravings, make us feel more full (resulting in less snacking), have consistent energy, and it's lower in calories. One of the reasons these foods positively impact us is due to the abundance of vitamins, minerals, healthy fats, and proteins they contain. If we want to lose some extra weight, it won't take long to see results once we start consistently having the first meal of the day packed with protein from meat or fish.

With regard to the next generation of hunters, consider the idea that breakfast is an important meal of the day. What if parents fed the next generation of hunters more nourishing foods rather than breakfast cereals? Numerous breakfast cereals contain vegetable/seed oils, refined grains/flour, processed sugars/artificial sweeteners, soy, and even glyphosate (weed killer, a.k.a. Roundup).[10] As mentioned previously, these ingredients, when consumed regularly, could potentially alter hormones, cause weight gain (fat), lead to behavioral problems, cause unnecessary inflammation, and activate the immune system. When regularly ingested, all of these ingredients have the potential to lead to worsened bodily and mental health. If you are a parent, do everything it takes to provide the next generation of hunters with better quality food so they can be healthier and thrive in life. Like sweet potato pancakes or scrambled eggs with avocado and raspberries.

Me with a black-tailed buck taken in mid-October on the Oregon coast at 11:30 a.m. in seventy-eight-degree weather.

I am driven to educate the next generation of hunters in understanding the importance of consuming nourishing foods after seeing this photo from when I was younger. In my teenage years, I believed

I could eat whatever I wanted and still be healthy because I kept reasonably skinny. Unfortunately, this is a misguided way of thinking. We are not immune to ill health just because we don't gain weight and look to be "healthy." My body was not healthy internally since I frequently ate packaged foods, drank processed protein shakes, and devoured low-quality foods like cereal. Now that I think about it, this makes sense because I always caught a cold, had trouble learning new material in school, slept poorly, and had acne (a sign of gut health problems).

DIETARY SUPPLEMENTS

It's important to think about our goals while using dietary supplements as they become more popular online for promoting better health through numerous advertisements and claims that look enticing. Consider the past few years. Did you take any dietary supplements? Have you actually succeeded in your goals with them? If so, that's fantastic! If you haven't, there may be an underlining reason for this. This is a factor that, in my opinion, can expedite your progress toward your goals if dealt with effectively. Let's take a closer look at this.

It is imperative that we understand what is meant by a "supplement." Supplement means to assist. Supplement does not mean replace. Before purchasing new dietary supplements, it's important to understand this differential and assess our own thought processes. Think about the motivating factors that led you to choose a certain dietary supplement. Is it a result of your doctor's advice after a blood test analysis? Is it because you saw a professional hunter who happens to be promoting the product in a magazine or on social media? Why did your close friend inform you of it? Was it a result of what they had heard on a podcast? These are all typical situations in which dietary supplements enter our lives.

Depending on our age, geographical location, health status, lifestyle, genetics, and, of course, the recommendation of our primary doctor, dietary supplements are frequently appropriate for particular areas of health and survival. In these situations, it seems reasonable to take a particular dietary supplement. We should be cautious when using the other reasons I listed for wanting to take a dietary supplement, though.

Imagine watching a TV commercial for a new fat-burning supplement. Now, attempt to control the temptation to buy before you jump to conclusions and place an order. Consider whether using that dietary supplement is really necessary. Will that product fulfill our needs? Are there potential side effects? Is it pricey? Possibly or not. Before making a decision, it is essential to check in with ourselves that we are already consistently making better lifestyle choices. This is why.

Even the highest-priced and most cutting-edge dietary supplements won't work as well if we don't frequently exercise, sleep poorly, consume alcohol regularly, eat more treats than nourishing foods, or let stress control our bodies and mind. The truth is that all dietary supplements perform better when we consistently make better lifestyle choices! Crazy, huh? This makes sense because a supplement's primary role is to assist. The key is assistance with healthy lifestyle choices that have already been made. If the proper lifestyle choices are not consistently made before taking the dietary supplement, the product's effectiveness is decreased, it doesn't give us the results we really want, and in many cases, the underlying cause of poor health is simply making poor lifestyle choices on a consistent basis. In this situation, using a dietary supplement is equivalent to relying on a

"Band-Aid" fix for a problem rather than addressing the underlying fundamental root causes of poor health or whatever it is we are attempting to improve. Daily dietary supplements might provide some advantages, but they won't come close to what we'd get by also maintaining a healthier lifestyle.

I can speak from personal experience when I say that I was a big proponent of using a range of dietary supplements when I was younger, including protein drinks, bars, and multivitamins. I did this because I believed in the claims made in the advertisements that ideal levels of health and fitness were assured and essential for vitality. You see, I was never encouraged to consider utilizing a dietary supplement after I had already prioritized eating better quality food, such as nourishing foods, for example.

Funny thing is, I still suffered from a lot of sicknesses at that time, felt lousy, had issues with my memory and learning, slept poorly, had bloating and low energy, and could not recover quickly from workouts. So, I decided to learn more, which gave me the idea to modify my perspective on dietary supplements. My current guiding philosophy is to consistently make healthier lifestyle choices, such as eating the nourishing foods mentioned before, as often as feasible. If I do this, most of my protein, vitamin, and mineral requirements will be satisfied.

There is a reason why some who consume large quantities of protein shakes still struggle to lose weight and reduce body fat. Making better lifestyle choices, such as consistently eating adequate protein from meat or fish and limiting snacking, as was already said, can help with this predicament. If this is a given, there is a strong chance we can move toward achieving our long-term goals and the physique we desire. I predict it won't take long, especially if we are honest about being consistent. Then, if interested, think about experimenting with a protein shake.

I believe there is less of a need to take any synthetic and artificial multivitamins made in a lab if a person bases their meals around nourishing foods like wild game, wild-caught fish, grass-fed meat, vegetables, and fruit because the majority of the vitamins and minerals listed in dietary supplements are present in those foods. In addition to being present in certain foods, these vitamins and minerals are also more natural (easier for our bodies to digest and use). This may help to explain why, since I changed my approach, I rarely get sick, feel great, sleep soundly, think clearly, never feel bloated, have a better physique, and recover quickly from training sessions.

If we don't eat nourishing food and make other healthy dietary decisions, supplements won't be as helpful in accomplishing our goals as they could be. The idea behind this is comparable to that of current pandemic vaccines or even flu shots. If we rely on these resources to protect us and keep us healthy when we get sick while ignoring the quality of our dietary habits and lifestyle choices, we are not in the greatest position. To be in a better position, it appears that, at the very least, better lifestyle choices ought to be made, such as getting enough sleep, working out frequently, cutting back on soda and alcohol, having a strong moral compass, spending time outside in the sunshine and fresh air, eating nourishing foods, lowering stress, not snacking, and so on. Experts refer to this as the preventative mindset. If these things are happening regularly, you can expect to: lessen health risks and limitations, enhance your immune system, and recover more quickly from sickness. After that, additional tools like a flu shot or vaccine can potentially aid us if we choose to use them. Wouldn't it be comforting to be healthier while a sickness, whether known or unknown, is spreading? Prevention is essential rather than waiting for something to happen to make a change or expecting that a tool will be created. Sometimes it's too late at that point.

If you're interested in dietary supplements, ensure you're primed with this preventative health approach. Then, consider contacting your primary doctor to find out which aspects of your internal health need to be improved and whether it would be beneficial to include a supplement for your unique needs.

Consider learning about, testing with, and researching the many dietary supplements that can give you the "help" you need for optimum health if you want to take control of the situation. Experiment with different dietary supplements for your individual needs and self-reflect on how your body and mind feel. Keep in mind that each person will probably react differently.

Since the supplement industry is largely unregulated in the United States, it is vital to confirm that the company and products we are consuming are from a reliable source. Look for supplements that list all the ingredients, how much of each there are, and what each one does.

In the end, be fully accountable and verify that you are consistently making better lifestyle choices (such as those detailed in this book) before thinking about using a dietary supplement. If this happens, our physical and mental health can improve, and the dietary supplement we intend to take may work more effectively. Now we are getting somewhere.

HEALTH TESTS

The next level is to start investigating different health tests, assuming that improved lifestyle choices, particularly dietary ones, are being made consistently and that you are beginning to experiment with dietary supplements for your particular needs. The rapid growth and advancement of the health sciences field and technology are among its most intriguing features. A person can now complete a wide range of various blood, saliva, stool, and gene tests if they want to enhance many different aspects of their health. With the help of these many tests, we can better understand what each of us is required to do to maintain our health as we age. We will undoubtedly be in a better position to take advantage of more opening days and hunting opportunities if we make lifestyle changes that better suit our own needs.

Our biological age, risk of developing diseases, vitamin D levels, hormone levels, reactivity to various foods, the functioning of our gut and other organs, and many other variables can all be assessed by specific health tests. The important thing is to actually implement the lifestyle changes required to precisely meet our individual needs once we have had a chance to study the results.

Similar to the idea of dietary supplements, be sure that the company and the test you want to experiment with come from a reputable and trustworthy source. Since they will have samples from you, this is essential. Make sure you read the test guidelines in detail and that the test sample is kept in utmost confidentiality.

Seeking out ways to improve our health using various health tests may make life itself more worthwhile and meaningful due to functioning at a higher level physically, mentally, and spiritually.

Ways #23–32 to Age Better and Prevent Disease

23. Consume a variety of nourishing foods based on your individual needs.
24. Eat till you are content, not stuffed.
25. Incorporate a treat allowance to maintain balance for your specific needs.
26. Be consistent (patient) and accountable (honest) with your dietary habits.
27. Aim for drinking filtered water based on thirst or half your body weight in ounces.
28. Incorporate unrefined salt into your meals and your water bottle.
29. Incorporate the 16:8 method.
30. Minimize snacking and eat less often.
31. Incorporate dietary supplements for your individual needs.
32. Explore blood, saliva, stool, and gene tests.

CHAPTER 4

OVERLOOKED AND UNDERVALUED

Better Sleep Is Natural Energy

Numerous elements, both in-season and off-season, can naturally increase our energy levels. A crucial aspect that is frequently neglected but can help with natural energy is getting good quality sleep. You may remember hearing when you were younger that eating the right foods and exercising were healthy habits. Which they are. But for some reason, few people are informed of the significance of sleep and its impact on our health and well-being. For natural energy, superior health, and experiencing more opening days and hunting opportunities, sleep is a critical component of this *Healthspan* equation. The quality of our sleep appears to have a substantial impact on every organ in our body, particularly the brain. It is undoubtedly a crucial part of our DNA wiring that protects the functions of all our cells.

> A fully charged battery works well in my headlamp. A partially charged battery is impaired and creates flickering, which is inefficient. Same idea behind our sleep and brain.

To climb up in that tree stand while in Canada for that bear hunt or make it to the top of the knoll for glassing Mule deer in Colorado, you most likely have had to rise up early to leave in the morning or walk out of the mountains late at night, which interfered with your sleep. There are instances when we have no control over what happens, such as when you and your pals spent the entire night carrying Roosevelt elk quarters out of the Oregon coast canyon. We can't complain about not getting any rest while we were carrying large packs of quality meat throughout the night until five in the morning.

There is no way to predict what might occur on the hunting trip that could prevent us from getting any sleep. Even so, there are still aspects and habits of sleep that are important to be aware of. We can, at the very least, consider our own sleeping habits and how well we sleep during the off-season to make improvements. To put people's sleep troubles in perspective, consider the fact that millions of people consult doctors about their sleep problems. If you fall into this category and you hunt, there are ways to acquire the rejuvenating sleep you so badly want; just stick with me.

A positive step in the right direction is strengthening our ability for self-awareness regarding our sleep habits and how they influence us. In some respects, we can get away with bad lifestyle choices while we are younger that affect our capacity to sleep and still function on a regular basis. At least, that is how I felt when I slept poorly in high school and college. It's a misconception that adults are less capable of getting good sleep than children. From what I have gathered, it is not necessarily that adults have fewer skills to sleep well; it's that adults often develop poor sleeping habits over time that have put them in that position of sleep dysfunction.

For instance, one of the challenges many adults face with poor sleep is that they wake up in the middle of the night to use the bathroom and then find it difficult to fall back asleep. This is one opportunity related to sleep that we might be able to influence potentially. Prepare yourself beforehand for a liquid consumption plan. Be done ingesting any liquids around 7:00 p.m. if you intend to go to bed around 9:00 p.m. To reduce the likelihood of waking up in the middle of the night, try to wait until just before going to bed to urinate one final time to clear everything.

Let's say we still need to wake up in the middle of the night to urinate. Using a phone light or teeny flashlight to navigate our way into the bathroom is a wise course of action to take into consideration in this case. To have as little light contact with your eyes as possible, turn as much of the light away from you as possible. Instead of turning on the bathroom light, choose this. Our brain and body begin to think it's time to wake up and move when that bathroom light reaches our eyes. This makes it really difficult to fall asleep again. Because of the way hormones are dispersed, exposure to bathroom light can have a detrimental effect on the rest of the night as well as our next day's mood, intelligence, behavior, memory, thoughts, and emotions. Have a strategy in place if you must urinate in the middle of the night. By doing this, you can lessen the difficulty of falling asleep again, which is a prime example of how to strategically position yourself as you get older to obtain that high-quality sleep.

SLEEP DEPRIVATION

If you have ever experienced sleep deprivation, you are aware of how harmful it is. It has the potential to fundamentally alter your personality and transform you on many levels, and not for the better. Our health may suffer profoundly as a result of it. For instance, a lack of sleep could potentially suppress our immune system, which in turn activates some of our genes that are linked to inflammation and disease.[11] We can somewhat change our genetic makeup by sleeping well or poorly. Our sleep quality can determine a myriad of factors:

- How patient we are on a stalk of an Aoudad sheep
- How efficiently we digest our food
- The quality of our training session
- How well we aim at that Axis deer
- How insightful we can be
- How careful we are when breaking down the wild game
- How well we manage our emotions
- How prone we are to snacking
- How well we can cope with stress
- How well we retain newly learned information
- How alert and focused we are

All these circumstances can show us how the quality of our sleep beforehand could dictate how we operate. You might discover that on various instances during some of your hunts, a mistake was made that just so happened to occur after a bad night's sleep. Lack of sleep can affect a hunter's concentration, leading to mistakes in shot placement, accidents, and other problems. Think about how you feel when you get to work and during the day throughout the off-season. As the afternoon wears on, it could become more difficult to concentrate. Lack of sleep, among other things, impacts our ability to focus without being distracted.

The quality of our sleep impacts our ability to learn from prior experiences and avoid making the same mistake while firing an arrow. With a good night's sleep, we can learn from our past mistakes, improve as archery hunters, and permanently imprint new experiences in our memories. Without a doubt, not getting enough sleep impairs our brain's capacity for memory, learning, and decision-making.

A rested brain is better equipped to handle more challenging conditions. This is one of the reasons why, when sleep-deprived, we often go for the easiest solution, which involves less work. You can get more driven and become more like a *super hunter* by pursuing high-quality sleep. For instance, obtaining a good night's sleep prior might make you more likely (mentally tough) to trek to the top of that high-altitude mountain to find that Rocky Mountain goat you spotted, even if you're physically fatigued. Though we can't control everything during hunting, we can become more conscious of specific facets of sleep and take advantage of those times when we do have more control on the hunt and set ourselves up for physical and mental success to be dialed in for the chosen pursuit.

Consider the last time you had trouble sleeping during the off-season. When speaking to a person, was it harder to put words and sentences together? Word mistakes are a subtle sign of insufficient sleep because the brain needs sleep to recharge completely.

Additionally, those who don't get enough sleep are more likely to be emotionally reactive, quickly irritated, and pessimistic. All elements to be mindful of during meetings at work, interactions with a significant other, etc. In fact, as a new parent who was aware of this, I made sure to create a "reminder sheet" of what to anticipate while sleep-deprived so that I could avoid developing these negative traits, especially waking up repeatedly throughout the night to change a diaper. Naturally, practicing "diaper mock-ups" months in advance aids in keeping our minds on point when we're tired, but that's a different story for another time. Getting adequate sleep each night is essential for maintaining brain health, mental stability, and behavior over the course of one's lifetime.

Here's something thought-provoking to contemplate. In 2007, the World Health Organization designated working nights as a "probable carcinogen."[12] Could this classification result from the disruption to sleep and waking cycles that night-shift workers experience? It very well could be. No question that not getting enough sleep and being exposed to artificial light at night (more on this) affect the immune system and hormones, which might negatively affect their health and the quality of their work. It is crucial that you improve your lifestyle choices if you work a night shift in order to lessen any potential negative consequences.

Consistent Sleep Deprivation and Poor-Quality Sleep Could *Potentially* Lead To:

- Reduced immune system functioning
- Increased depression
- Less likely to apologize when wrong
- Increased chronic stress
- Less driven
- Increased anxiety
- Less productivity
- Chronic inflammation
- More cravings
- Quick to anger
- Increased irritability
- Decreased logical thought
- Joint pain
- Jumps to conclusions quickly
- Dysfunction of oral and gut health
- Greater chance of consuming poor-quality foods and beverages
- Increased chances for catching a cold and flu
- Increased risk for type 2 diabetes
- More susceptible to having a poor moral compass
- Teeth grinding
- Causes chronic diseases to spread at a faster rate throughout the body
- Dark circles under the eyes
- Increased risk for cancer
- Increased risk for cardiovascular disease
- Poor self-control
- Emotional instability
- Lack of focus
- Increased risk for Dementia and Alzheimer's
- Less self-awareness
- Migraines
- Reduced muscular strength and endurance
- Easily distracted
- Impaired reproductive system (alters fertility)
- Decreases verbal comprehension
- Increased rate of lying
- Hot flashes
- Less inspiring
- Hormone imbalance
- Weight gain
- Impairment of memory and learning
- Less happy
- Apnea
- Domestic abuse (verbal and physical)
- Gossiping and complaining about others
- Less likely to train
- Less energy
- Becoming a zombie and starting the apocalypse

Many factors from a lack of sleep can lead to illness and imbalance. Every major organ, tissue, and cell in our body becomes ill when we don't get enough sleep. Sleep deprivation can stem from various reasons, but it's important to know that there are things we can do to lessen its impact and the risk that it will happen to us. Insomnia is one of the primary causes of sleep deprivation for many people. Let's look at it.

INSOMNIA

Insomnia is seen as having difficulty falling asleep and staying asleep in relation to rehashing the past, stressing about the present, or worrying about the future. Many people can develop brief acute (short-term) insomnia. Chronic (long-term) insomnia is the point at which we need to draw the line and take a stand. Chronic insomnia may be linked to cardiovascular disease, asthma, headaches, gastrointestinal issues, thyroid dysfunction, Parkinson's disease, and arthritis.[13]

Chronic insomnia typically results from bad sleeping habits, work-related stress, relationship problems, financial concerns, painful memories, and trauma. All these aspects can be addressed and perhaps even improved upon when we create a strategic plan.

According to what I have observed, stress is by far one of the main causes of chronic insomnia, which keeps people up all night. Unfortunately, stress can negatively affect the quantity and quality of our total sleep. Here is what could happen. When something at work is about to happen, for example, we may feel stressed for a specific reason. This can lead to poor sleep, which causes our bodies to potentially have a stress response due to the bad sleep, which could then cause the stress to escalate. If we don't strive to stop it, this downward trend might never cease.

If you fall into this category, please don't give up and accept chronic insomnia as normal; there are tools available that could help your current position, regardless of how severe it is. For instance, if you start to have an anxiety attack or a roller coaster of emotions engulf you brought on by stress, think about code words or numbers that can help you reflect on your thoughts at that precise moment and determine if they are significant or not. When things seem to be going wrong or awful, keep in mind that you are in control and have the inner strength and capacity to manage your thoughts and emotions. You have the fortitude to make things seem less daunting. You have what it takes to handle these circumstances by using a methodical plan followed by ongoing practice. Here are four examples of the codes I use to reframe my thoughts when I start to get a nagging sense of stress-related anxiety to help you better understand what I mean:

- **Ninety-two:** When I am ninety-two years old, will I be thinking about it?
- **Space:** Is it significant in the grand scheme of the universe and time?
- **Owen:** Some are in far more challenging positions than I am in (more on this later).
- **Creation:** Watch a ladybug to see how it simply lives. Count raindrops on a tree.

It is well worth the time and effort to develop a plan with code words or numbers that you can use at anytime, especially before night, to decompress. It is a reliable source of inner strength to provide yourself with for preventing and overcoming anxiety.

Also, refer back to the chronic stress section in Chapter 1 for the strategies that can help you release stress. Use one or more for that nagging anxiety if it does manage to penetrate and overwhelm your body and mind to the point where it becomes difficult to swallow (tight throat), and your pulse rate becomes uncontrollable. Examine the times in your life when it feels that your anxiety is still present. Take time to think about what thoughts and information is entering your eyes, ears, and mind. Reduce the time you spend reading and scrolling through social media; pay less attention to other people's opinions and expectations (more on this later); stop worrying so much about your appearance; stop listening to negative music or news; stop being around people who complain, are mean, or are unkind, etc. All of these actions are changeable. You have the power to change your current position.

It's crucial to understand the relationship between our ability to sleep and the effects that anxiety may have on us. A restless night could possibly cause our anxiety levels to increase the following day significantly.[14] However, getting good quality sleep can minimize anxiety brought on by stress. We must break the cycle. Take charge, put some thought into a strategy, and realize that we can live our lives better if we take the reins and understand that every day presents an opportunity for growth and transformation. After a few months, weeks, or possibly even days of making changes to your mental health and sleep habits, I predict you will experience fewer days and nights of anxious thoughts and disturbed sleep. Let's cover a few categories in relation to sleep that are important to be aware of.

NATURAL LIGHT > ARTIFICIAL LIGHT

As time passes on, it appears that as a society, we are being exposed to more artificial light produced by technology and less natural light from the outside. Is this in favor of our health? Possibly not.

In fact, exposure to natural light from the outside helps to keep our hormones in check, maintain proper energy levels, ensure strong mental health, and promote good sleep.

The focus for artificial light exposure doesn't need to be so we eliminate it completely. The timing of our technology use is what has to be emphasized, particularly in the context of how well we sleep. For instance, the body's natural release of melatonin may be inhibited and delayed if exposed to artificial light from devices like a TV, computer, phone, or even ceiling lights just before bedtime. Melatonin is critical in preparing us for sound sleep and bolstering our immune systems. The preceding example of how we wake up in the middle of the night to use the bathroom is crucial to our sleeping habits because of this.

However, I'm not suggesting we never watch another episode of our preferred hunting show. Periodic use of the TV, computer, or phone before bed is okay; excessive usage has to be limited, especially if we have difficulties sleeping. If, like me, you enjoy watching hunting programs on TV, think about investing in blue light-blocking eyewear. With this approach, we can protect our eyes from potentially harmful artificial light exposure. This raises the likelihood that we can fall asleep more efficiently.

Another way to modify technology to work in our favor with regard to sleep is to change the display on our phones and computer to red light and/or warmer colors. The more closely these substitutes resemble a real sunset, the more effectively our hormones, brain, and body can respond to them. The closer our environment is to a natural sunset before bed, the better we sleep.

Avoiding the temptation to check social media and emails immediately before bed or right after waking up and placing your phone in a location other than your bedroom could help you get better sleep. Having images and information from our phones enter our minds just before going to sleep or immediately after waking up may subtly affect our mood, thoughts, and emotions. When you open your eyes, turn down the phone's invitation to scroll. Start your day off right by getting outside (regardless of the weather), training, stretching, reading a book, shooting your bow, conversing with others, and other things when you wake up. This is a crucial concept for the next generation of hunters to understand because too much screen time at certain times, such as immediately before bed and right when you wake up, may result in poor sleep and future mental health issues.

Spend at least fifteen minutes outside in the morning (sunrise), midday, and just before dark (sunset) without your phone to ensure that your body and mind are exposed to natural light. Do your best to find opportunities to be outdoors and exposed to natural light as frequently as you can while you're awake, whether you're sitting, standing, or walking. More exposure to natural light means we can stay awake better because melatonin levels are lower.[15] Better physical, mental, and spiritual health are thereby ensured.

Me with a 225-pound bear I took at thirty-two yards during our backcountry bow hunt for elk.

I began to appreciate how strong and durable a well-designed broadhead is at this point. With my Kudupoint Broadhead, I successfully took down this bear with a well-placed frontal shot, which had less than a ten-second expiration. It's a blessing to have tools that perform when needed.

As I look at this picture, I'm reminded of how this lifestyle involves a lot of exposure to natural light. One of the reasons why many hunters, including myself, say they sleep pretty well while out hunting is the exposure to natural light we receive first thing in the morning, during the day, and just before bed. Exposure to natural light improves our potential for high-level physical and mental performance throughout the awake day. This a valuable lesson to remember and put to use during the off-season.

MEAL TIMING

If you remember, I briefly noted that eating at the same time of day while on a hunt could be fairly difficult with the number of variables to consider. Every day poses new challenges and obstacles when we least expect that are frequently beyond our control. However, it's still pivotal to be more aware of our meal timing in relation to a hunt. Let's paint a scenario to convey what I mean. Imagine you are hunting for Tahr in New Zealand. On this ten-day quest, the last three days, you had seen relatively little activity. In other words, we have a little bit more control over when we eat. Okay, in this case, it could be a good idea to eat most of your meals earlier in the day rather than later in the evening, just before going to bed. Why? Read on.

If you ever experience morning grogginess or a lack of energy because you toss and turn or wake up frequently during the night, there may be a reason for poor sleep quality. And that is eating dinner just before going to bed.

A portion of the blood in our body shifts to the gut after eating a meal to help with digestion and absorption of the food. We want our blood flow during sleep to be predominantly distributed to and directed toward our brain and the rest of our body to manage the numerous hormones and processes required to aid recovery. All of which result in better quality sleep and internal balance. We risk interfering with the body's natural mechanisms by eating just before bed. This is why, if at all possible, we should strive to finish our last meal or bite of food at least a few hours before going to bed. If we eat dinner right before bed, there is a higher likelihood that we won't get a good night's sleep. This increases the chances that we won't be as patient the next day when placing a stalk, that we'll tire more quickly when sprinting up a mountain, that we'll get frustrated more easily, and other factors.

Here is an example of how we might modify this scenario to work in our favor. First, eat more of your meals in the morning and throughout the day, provided that you have control over the factors. Try your best to have dinner earlier if you know you'll be leaving camp at 5:00 p.m. for a hunt and returning to camp much later. This strategy aids in better sleep because it gives us a longer period without eating before bedtime since we won't need to eat when we return. There's a strong chance that if we use this technique, our morning could get off to a very different start. Different in a positive way.

When we are out hunting, countless things outside our control ultimately dictate when we eat our last meal and when we go to bed. Just work around what happens throughout your hunting trip. Then, when it's the off-season, and you have a better chance of having more control over your schedule and other things, at the very least, try to figure out how to ensure that there is a long period of time between your last meal and when you go to bed. When we wait at least a few hours after our last meal to go to bed, there may be a lower risk of breast and prostate cancer.[16]

PILLS

There is always a fine line when talking about pills in general. It is appropriate to take the precise medications that your primary doctor has recommended to help you function better. At other times, such as when we visit the grocery store to purchase over-the-counter medicines, we must exercise caution. The issue is that instead of self-reflection and awareness of what can be the origin of discomfort or issue, we merely focus on the symptoms. Consider a person who takes nonsteroidal anti-inflammatory drugs (NSAIDs) to treat a symptom like a headache. In this case, the discomfort can be managed, but the underlying cause for the headache may still exist. By addressing the headache's cause, the underlying problem, such as having improper posture, dehydration, or letting stress take over can be resolved. Once the underlying root cause is determined and resolved, we can lower the dosage of these pills. You might wonder how this relates to sleep. You'll see.

Taking pills regularly, such as anti-inflammatories, when they are not absolutely necessary might have detrimental impacts on our health, also known as side effects. For instance, it has been shown that aspirin and ibuprofen, when taken before bed, might decrease melatonin levels, raise the frequency of awakenings, and impair the quality of our sleep, interfering with our ability to sleep properly.[17] By itself, ibuprofen may also worsen digestive problems and stimulate the immune system, which in turn triggers a number of inflammatory processes while we sleep. So, while taking ibuprofen may temporarily help our headaches, there is a chance that it may also cause us to have sleep and other health problems.

Many factors can lead to the use of anti-inflammatories when hunting. Consider the situation where you are glassing for Fallow deer in Australia, and you are experiencing excruciating pain in your lower spine due to a recent surgery. Use as necessary in this instance. However, if you have more infrequent symptoms of discomfort, such as occasional gas, bloating, or a stomachache from something you ate, examine what may be irritating your digestive system and making it harder for you to get a good night's sleep whether on the hunt or at home. We could perhaps be able to alleviate these symptoms by discovering the cause. A cause like that freeze-dried meal that included vegetable and seed oils, or the fact that we frequently eat at restaurants. If using anti-inflammatories is our only choice due to not being able to pinpoint the source of the issue, and they are needed to help with the unmanageable pain and discomfort, then so be it. We don't necessarily have to avoid them all our lives. However, it could be a good idea to reconsider our dependence on them because there might be other solutions out there that are less harmful to our health and have fewer side effects. Always ask yourself whether there is a better alternative and consider why you are taking them.

Over-the-counter sleep aids could help you sleep, but they can also potentially lead to negative consequences, including daytime forgetfulness, sluggish reactions, and grogginess, to mention a few. Fixing one problem could lead to many more, as in the case of TV commercials for these pills. Another common product is taking over-the-counter melatonin to help promote sleep. Melatonin supplements for sleep have certain benefits, but taking too much of them may interfere with our bodies' natural melatonin levels. The most crucial thing is to ensure that melatonin and other hormones have the best opportunity to be naturally balanced by exposing yourself to more natural light from outside in the morning, midday, and late afternoon and less artificial light before bed.

No matter which pill you take, ask yourself why. Try to determine the root of the issue, if at all possible. Find out if there is another approach to get the desired outcome.

ALERTNESS AND DRIVING

In the hunting community, there isn't enough discussion about sleep and driving. I have to travel far to go hunting at times, as do many other individuals. It's important to understand that even one night of insufficient sleep will significantly reduce general awareness, which can make it challenging for us to drive safely. Driving while sleep-deprived could be just as dangerous as driving while intoxicated in terms of how our brain is affected.[18]

Therefore, it is essential for us to acquire adequate sleep to prepare ourselves for a long drive to a hunting spot. If you're too exhausted to keep going, it could be a better idea to pull over at a rest stop, where you can sleep in your car or book a room at a hotel. No matter how much time you save and how much more time you get to hunt, it is never safe for you or other drivers to drive when sleepy. Please be well-rested before traveling to your hunting location and returning home.

Roadside advice: avoid social media, reading, responding to texts, and checking emails while driving as best as you can. All of these tasks are distractions that could take our focus off of driving and lead to unfortunate events when we least expect them. Having a plan of attack for these habits would look like taking care of them all before we leave or when we are done driving. Note how each of these actions relates to the attention-stealing effects of technology.

ALCOHOL

Periodic alcohol usage is okay if desired, but excessive drinking on a regular basis, especially before bed, can be harmful to our health on a variety of levels, including how well we sleep. If we regularly consume too much alcohol before bed, it may cause sleep disturbances and even insomnia.[19] Brief awakenings might partly explain this during the night brought on by disruptions in the sleep cycle. Consider drinking alcohol in the late afternoon or early evening if you want to (and are of legal drinking age).

It's important, in my opinion, to identify our goals and the reasons behind our alcohol consumption. Perhaps you're enjoying a whisky toast with your friends to the large Caribou you harvested in Greenland. I say go ahead and take a sip. If you feel like you need it to escape from your job or life and are stressed out, maybe think twice. Alcohol consumption may potentially increase the risk of dehydration, increased anxiety, weight gain, gastrointestinal problems, and hormonal imbalance, in addition to affecting some brain processes and disrupting sleep. Even if we can forget about the stressful scenario from the previous day, the stressor may still be there since we didn't deal with the root of the problem or use strategies that could assist us in separating ourselves from it. This can result in physical and mental impairment from alcohol the day after drinking, as well as a continuing stressor for us to handle.

Unfortunately, using alcohol as a quick way to deal with stress, worry, or depression will never be a long-term solution. We may feel better in a short period of time, but it's only tricking us into thinking it's helping us resolve the problem. Furthermore, it could cause us to frequently overindulge and, unexpectedly, develop an addiction. Then, after repeated use, it becomes quite challenging to stop using it since the addiction maintains a solid grip on us.

If you or someone you care about is battling an addiction to alcohol or another harmful substance, there is hope. Ask for guidance from a professional such as an alcohol counselor, as soon as possible.

You might hear just what you need from an alcohol counselor to make a difference in your life. My uncle Linden was an alcohol counselor and found it incredibly meaningful to witness lives transformed like a rebirth—it was common. After speaking with a professional, think about exploring and going deep inside yourself to uncover the underlying causes of why you decided to overindulge. If you give yourself enough time to reflect, you might be able to identify some potential root causes. Will this be easy? It will not be. Actually, it will be among the toughest challenges to overcome. The truth is that it is worthwhile to put in the effort and time to take on a challenge such as this, especially one that, when achieved, can make you feel the proudest of yourself, ever. If nobody has told you, you have the abilities; now is the time to rise up and prove to the world you have the skills to overcome anything. The life you truly want is waiting for you, so fasten your seatbelt and get going.

Once the root cause or causes have been discovered, you might want to think about applying some of the strategies in this book to help you begin to distance yourself from them. Alcohol abuse has a negative effect on our internal health, takes our attention away from the source of the issue, and accelerates aging. I don't find any of those to be enticing. The approaches we discussed in Chapter 1 are more effective ways to manage stress.

I've seen plenty of horrible situations and incidents involving alcohol. It can cause everything from friends to lose their lives, addictions, car accidents, ending long-term relationships, domestic violence (physical and verbal abuse), loss of career, etc. Actually, I nearly dropped out of college my first year because of turning to alcohol (don't worry, I found the reason). Unfortunately, sometimes we have to experience something negative before we decide to stop drinking.

We might get lucky and have the opportunity to change our habits. Other times not so much.

If one were to evaluate all of alcohol's advantages against its disadvantages, it would be obvious that the disadvantages outweighed the advantages. Recognize that alcohol is simply for temporary enjoyment and is not necessary for health or survival. Given this, make an effort to limit your weekly drinking from zero to two drinks. I normally only have one glass of red wine every two weeks, most often when on a date with my wife. But when I follow my preconception protocol, I hardly seldom, if ever, really touch it (more on this in a future book).

I'm not advocating that you abstain from alcohol entirely when you go hunting with friends. I'm encouraging you to keep control by restraining the want from overindulging and that it's important to work on raising your degree of self-awareness regarding the reasons behind your consumption. I want to be a positive role model for the next generation of hunters, don't you? More drinks or more opening days and hunting opportunities? You choose.

CAFFEINE INFLUENCE AND TIMING

You won't find a line that urges you to abstain from coffee for the rest of your life, so don't worry. But what you'll see is a plan for making sure we use it to our advantage in terms of sleep quality. Let's first determine how dependent we are on caffeine. Give up caffeine for fifteen days. I am aware that this seems like a terrible idea. Let me explain, though. To gauge how our energy and sleep are functioning, I propose taking a break from consuming any kind of caffeine. If it's challenging to function without caffeine for those fifteen days, we might need to change our sleeping habits. You can reintroduce caffeine if you'd like once you've adjusted your sleep habits (stay tuned for strategies), as long as you maintain your newly improved sleeping habits. Be aware that there are other caffeine-free options you could consume in place of coffee during this fifteen-day caffeine-free period, including bone broth, tea, kefir, and lemon water, all of which have numerous health benefits.

Let's assume that our sleeping habits are under control, everything is going well, and you can resume enjoying your morning cup of coffee while hunting for White-tailed bucks in Wisconsin. The next step is realizing that when we drink, it can affect how we feel during the day and the following night. A good rule of thumb is to refrain from drinking anything caffeinated, like coffee, for at least a few hours after waking up. This enables our bodies to smoothly transition into the morning and day with balanced hormones without the interference of an external influence (caffeine) on our body and brain, decreasing the likelihood of an afternoon energy collapse. If you usually wake up at 6:00 a.m. and have a cup of coffee, think about trying to wait until at least 8:00 a.m. to have your coffee. Consume water (preferably filtered) with unrefined salt first, then your coffee. I've had great success with this approach regarding daily energy, mood, thinking, emotions, and sleep.

ALARM CLOCKS

When that alarm goes off, think about how you feel during the off-season. It might be worthwhile experimenting with an alternative alarm clock design if a noise-based alarm clock causes your pulse rate to increase, followed by a grumpy mood. Noise-based alarm clocks could cause our blood pressure and heart rate to increase, which imitates a minor "fight or flight" response and makes us feel anxious. Panicked mornings are not the best way to get up. Try using a sunrise simulation clock for a less anxious, more natural start to the morning.

Here are a few compelling reasons why using a sunrise simulation clock might be useful. It first simulates a natural waking brought on by the sunrise. Some claim that because it helps our bodies feel alive and promotes robust mental health, our DNA craves the early wake-up from the light of the surroundings. Remember how lovely the sunrises and mornings are when you're out hunting. I know I do. The pink, yellow, orange, and red morning color hues as the sun is gradually rising over the mountain seem very beautiful. In the backcountry, when I pause to observe and take in the morning, I feel as though my spirit and energies are being replenished. There is a reason why exposing our eyes and brain to those lovely colors and light feels so nice. Our DNA hungers for a morning transition such as a sunrise.

In addition, since we frequently use our phones as alarm clocks, we can now leave them in a room other than the one in which we sleep. When our phone is in a different room than the one we sleep in, we are less likely to begin our day getting sucked into it. Try using a sunrise-simulation clock, and be prepared for a dramatic improvement in your behavior, mental health, and energy levels.

NAPPING

Ask yourself whether you ever feel you need to sleep in on the weekends during the off-season. If so, this may be a subtle sign that your body needs to rest and recover after a week of inadequate sleep. To obtain more hours Monday through Friday, it may be wise to go to bed earlier in this situation. Then, once you've caught up on your sleep, try to be more consistent about waking up at the same time every day to keep your body and brain in balance, regardless of what day of the week it is. Let's say it's challenging for you to go to bed sooner because of your schedule, work, and family commitments. Herein lies a useful tool: napping. Consider taking a nap if you feel like you need a quick recharge because you don't feel rested or you didn't get enough sleep.

It will probably be quite challenging to nap at work, unless your place of employment offers a lounge area designated just for naps (yes, they do exist). Therefore, a good strategy could be to get in an afternoon nap on the weekends and wake up at the same time every day, as it is more difficult to leave work during the week for a quick nap. Taking a nap is similar to charging your phone. If you plug your phone in for ten minutes, you might get 7 percent more charge to your battery. Imagine that a ten-minute nap might give you 7 percent more energy and focus. A nap can be healthy for the body and the mind if it is taken at an appropriate time.

A nap's duration can vary depending on the individual and how tired they are. A typical rule of thumb is to limit our nap to forty-five minutes and take it between 12:00 and 3:00 p.m. to lessen the possibility that it may disrupt our evening sleep the following night. Napping between those times of day may improve alertness, patience, energy, and learning abilities—all of which are tested while hunting and in everyday life.

My father used to nap frequently in the field during the archery season. He used to talk about waking up feeling like he had hit the reset button because he was so energized. As soon as he opened his eyes, he also managed to harvest elk with his longbow while seated against a tree. How he harvested many elk after waking up from a nap has always baffled me. My father would sleep against a tree while an elk herd would frequently, and I mean frequently, feed nearby. I'm unsure if he knew where to sleep in case a herd passed by or if he had a lucky rock.

I've been thinking about these stories, and I'm beginning to think that when we take a nap in the woods, our internal energy changes from "pursue" to "relax." The elk or other wild game we are after might not be able to feel our energy because it is showing signs of relaxation, so they might not see it as a threat. As a result, elk herds would frequently feed nearby as my father dozed off. I'm sure you can find a few moments throughout your hunt to take a nap, just like my father did. You might have revitalized energy as a result, and you might also get the chance to hunt your preferred wild game right then and there.

THE BUSY LIFE DILEMMA

There is a movement in society right now that supports the idea that we should work more to achieve our goals. Unquestionably a good idea to encourage individuals to work harder in their life. However, some of the better lifestyle choices we can make for our health, like obtaining sufficient sleep, are commonly neglected, for example, when we get overly focused on work.

In general, neglecting sleep and adopting poor lifestyle habits on a regular basis to get more work done during the off-season may not be the best option for our health in the long run. We must be conscious that putting our health at risk to work more could lead to health limitations developing sooner (refer back to potential health consequences of sleep deprivation), which would reduce our quality of life and reduce our ability to hunt. I think we can probably still complete work-related things in a certain amount of time while awake and still have a restful night's sleep.

Imagine writing down each and every minute of your day for a full week, from waking up to going to bed. Then, instead of making poor lifestyle choices and getting less sleep, you try to find some time that is not being used effectively and make the most of it. Get as much sleep as you need to feel refreshed, and finish everything for work and on your to-do list while you are up.

INDIVIDUAL NEEDS

Similar to the idea of the kind of foods we eat, there is no set number of hours of sleep that works for everyone. According to common consensus, most people require between seven and nine hours of sound sleep each night to promote total recovery and cell regeneration, which improves the body's systems. But make no mistake; some people have genes that allow them to get by on less sleep while maintaining health.

Everyone has somewhat different sleep needs; therefore, it's a good idea to visit a sleep specialist for an assessment to determine how many hours you need to sleep. The second-best option is to do your own experiments to establish what sleeping time frame you think provides you the most energy and clarity throughout the day.

You might require more restorative and higher-quality sleep if you begin to feel tired halfway through the morning to the point where it would be easy to fall back asleep. In this situation, try to stay up as much as possible and become increasingly exhausted throughout the day by engaging in some form of physical activity. Then, try to go to bed early and sleep longer.

I've compiled a list of strategies that might be worth trying if you frequently have difficulties falling asleep, wake up in the middle of the night, and do not feel refreshed during the day. A few of the listed strategies would be difficult to use when hunting. As a result, during the off-season, try to follow as many of them as you can. Every hunter ought to consider making sleep a priority. Here is a list of things to try out to obtain better sleep:

When You Wake Up (Morning Time)

1. Have a screen curfew (no screens) for at least thirty minutes when waking up—screens consisting of TV, computer, and phone (any human-made device with artificial light essentially).
2. Obtain natural light from outside (sunrise) for at least fifteen minutes. Go for a walk or sit outside.
3. For the last minute of your shower, make it cold.
4. Consume a glass of water (preferably filtered) with unrefined salt. Then, if you desire, wait a few hours before drinking coffee. Try your best not to overconsume it (evaluate how you feel) and avoid having it later than the afternoon.
5. Wait a few hours till you eat.

Throughout the Day

1. Obtain natural light from outside during midday for at least fifteen minutes.
2. Be physically active.
3. Stay hydrated with water (preferably filtered).
4. Utilize the 16:8 method and have consistent eating times.
5. Consume nourishing foods.

Before Bed (Nighttime)

1. Obtain natural light from outside before dark (sunset) for at least fifteen minutes.
2. Be done eating for at least two hours.
3. Be done drinking any liquids for at least two hours.
4. Utilize blue light-blocking glasses when watching TV.
5. Have a screen curfew (no screens) for at least thirty minutes before bed—screens consisting of TV, computer, and phone (any human-made device with artificial light essentially).
6. Try nasal breathing for twenty minutes with a cadence of five-second inhale, five-second hold, and five-plus second slow exhale (more on this in Chapter 5).
7. Read a tangible book (paper-based) while keeping light low and directed away from your face.
8. Static stretch for at least ten minutes.
9. Dim ceiling lights or utilize non-scented candles.
10. Take a warm bath/shower. Utilize Epsom salt in the bath.

Miscellaneous

1. Switch your phone and computer screen to red light/warmer colors.
2. Keep your bedroom temperature cool (60–67 degrees) and dark.
3. Try to have any and all devices with an electromagnetic field (TV, phone, computer, etc.) outside of your sleeping quarters. Turn phone notifications off.
4. Reduce direct contact with phones to prevent potential disruption of natural electrical frequencies.
5. Aim for seven to nine hours of good quality sleep.

6. Use a low pillow (more flat and less filling) to ensure proper spine alignment. A low pillow allows the brain's complete cellular regeneration to occur due to better blood flow—an excellent option for those with neck and back pain.
7. Aim for going to bed and waking up close to the same time every day.
8. Train around the same time every day and make sure your training session produces a sweat. Be physically active and exhaust yourself throughout the day.
9. If you take a nap, take it between 12:00 p.m.–3:00 p.m. (less than forty-five minutes).
10. Brush your teeth after each meal. Bonus points for flossing.
11. Switch your light bulbs to red light.
12. Invest in a sunrise simulation clock.
13. Invest in a grounding pad for sleeping (more on this in Chapter 5).
14. Invest in earplugs and a sleep mask.
15. Invest in mouth tape.
16. Invest in a noisemaker with natural noises (ocean, stream, rainforest).
17. Invest in a self-cooling mattress and blanket.
18. Find ways to minimize chronic stress.
19. Develop code words or numbers to use for anxiety.
20. Morally, be a good person.

The more closely we adhere to these sleeping strategies, the greater the likelihood we can experience results. Do we have to adhere to these strategies perfectly every day? Of course not. What about trying to increase our consistency with these habits? Absolutely.

It's crucial to understand that creating a solid new sleeping habit could take weeks. Whatever your situation, stick to these strategies and try to be as consistent as possible. It pays off when you put in the work to set yourself up for success in feeling great now and in the future. We need to shoot arrows often to improve our chances of getting a good shot on that buck. When establishing improved sleeping habits, keep that thinking in mind. Let's stop feeling drowsy, worn out, and fatigued all the time. Now is the perfect time to discover how amazing this body, mind, and spirit can feel after a restful sleep.

> Hunters, get your sleep in. Deer never hit the snooze button; neither should you.

Ways #33–40 to Age Better and Prevent Disease

33. Go to bed and wake up close to the same time every day.
34. Have a screen curfew before bed and when you wake up.
35. Switch your phone and computer screen to red light/warmer colors.
36. Be done eating at least two hours before bed.
37. Get outside for natural light exposure first thing in the morning, during midday, and before dark.

38. Wait a few hours after waking before ingesting caffeine.

39. Aim for seven to nine hours of good quality sleep.

40. Develop code words or numbers to use for anxiety.

CHAPTER 5

KEEP IT SIMPLE

Breath, Stillness, and the Environment

After my father served in the Coast Guard during the Vietnam War, he became heavily involved in martial arts. At the age of five, he introduced me to a style of martial arts called Kajukenbo. My father, being quite high in the family tree of practitioners and a grandmaster under this branch, dedicated his whole life starting in the 1970s to expanding upon his technique and self-defense theories. He traveled the world, conducting seminars and collaborating with many prominent figures in the martial arts community. In fact, this lifestyle meant so much to him that he proposed to my mother that my middle name be named after one of the founders of Kajukenbo —Emperado. My mom agreed. Naturally, you can guess that I was going to immerse myself and my energies within this community that my family was so deeply involved with.

Being active in martial arts at a young age taught me many things, one of which was the value of the *breath*, not just for the physical body but also for the mind and spirit. Growing up, I regularly underwent intense training where my *breath* was tested at my father's martial arts school. If you think about it, the most important component for life and survival is the oxygen our bodies receive via our *breath*. One of the concepts that stuck with me to this very day in relation to the *breath* is the importance of nasal breathing.

NASAL BREATHING

We are aware that there are two ways to breathe. However, there is a distinction between the air entering through the mouth and entering through the nose regarding how they affect our health. Due to a number of factors, it appears that nasal breathing is healthier for us than mouth breathing. For starters, nasal breathing activates the appropriate respiratory muscles, which increases the efficiency with which oxygen reaches our brain, tissues, and cells. Try it for yourself. As you read these words now or the next time you're out hunting, take ten deep nasal breaths in and let each one out slowly through the nose. You might start to experience a slight sense of euphoria. Your body and mind are receiving a tremendous amount of oxygen, which is what is causing the wonderful feeling you are currently experiencing.

Me after a successful archery Rocky Mountain elk hunt.

The trip that provided the prior bear I mentioned also provided this photograph. Shortly after harvesting that bear, we got heavily into the elk. Elk hunting with a bow is a huge learning experience, and I appreciate it. Sometimes we lose sight of the opportunity we have to be out there when we make mistakes that would normally take ten years to make in eight days, as I did. From what I've learned, everything that happens, including the good, the bad, and the ugly, is a part of the process. You won't regret it if you persevere and try harder the next time.

During this journey, the stars must have been in sync because I was able to harvest this outstanding bull. Nasal breathing was one of the factors that helped me handle this situation. Most of my errors on this trip were caused, among other things, by improper breathing patterns that were too quick, chaotic, and overwhelming. I took several deep breaths in through my nose and exhaled slowly out of my nose before approaching this bull elk to regulate my breathing and heart rate better. It worked because it helped me become more at ease and relaxed so I could aim precisely. There are many moments and situations that are connected to some degree to how we breathe. Let's discuss a few of them.

Posture

Our everyday lifestyle habits, combined with the evolution of technology, have slowly but surely led to us being in poor postural positions. As was previously noted in Chapter 2, having good posture is essential for maintaining joint health, preventing injuries, and experiencing more opening days and hunting opportunities. Our breathing patterns are one of the factors frequently disregarded in relation to proper posture.

When we mouth breathe on a consistent basis, we over-engage certain skeletal muscles that can cause us to be in poor postural alignment. As a result, our neck and head muscles can tighten over time and raise the risk of developing headaches. Additionally, it can make us unconsciously hunch over, which is bad for our backs. However, we can minimize this by nasal breathing.

Start by becoming more upright when sitting, standing, and walking. Once you have ingrained that behavior, you must perfect your tongue placement. To begin, place your tongue on the roof of your mouth and flatten it until the tip of it is in contact with the rear of your front teeth. Close your mouth, keeping your teeth slightly apart but not clamped. This part is essential. The explanation is that our tongue is made up of a collection of muscles that, when placed in a better position (on the roof of our mouth), can stimulate the muscles surrounding our throat and airway, realigning and supporting the positioning of our jaw and head. Based on how our muscles work, our bones are pulled into the positions they are in. Therefore, greater neck and head alignment may result from activating the appropriate postural muscles through nasal breathing with better tongue placement. Our posture and ability to receive oxygen are both improved by greater alignment.

The diaphragm and the intercostal muscles are other aspects of nasal breathing and better posture to be aware of. The intercostals are the spaces between each rib, and the diaphragm is beneath our ribs. Our rib cage and belly can fully expand to allow the most oxygen to pass through when the diaphragm and intercostal muscles are activated to a greater degree by nasal breathing. Our mid to upper spine can be better aligned in a stronger postural position to be more balanced and upright when sitting, standing, and walking once our rib cage and belly move oxygen more efficiently.

We can climb up those mountains after wild game without becoming as exhausted as quickly if we are more upright, have better posture, and have better breathing mechanics. I can personally attest to this. In the off-season, I focus on nasal breathing during my training sessions, which allows my upper spine to feel more upright and allows my hips to carry a heavier pack while hunting rather than my back.

Training

I've implemented the idea of nasal breathing during training sessions into the high school and collegiate sports programs I currently assist. When riding a fan bike and running, I instruct student-athletes to close their mouths and breathe via their noses. I have seen astonishing fitness benefits that are comparable to training or hunting at higher altitudes.

For instance, the next time you decide to run, perform pushups, use a rower, complete lunges, or go on a hike, nasal breathe throughout the activity to increase oxygen absorption and engage the right breathing muscles. Initially, it may be difficult to breathe via your nose when engaging in any activity, particularly if the intensity is high. However, it can get easier the more you do it. Due to increased oxygen levels and improved circulation, you might reach a new level of fitness and mental clarity once you are consistent.

With my student-athletes, I also integrate another breathing element in training, which is to have them carry out particular exercises while holding their breath. For instance: I instruct the football players to take in a deep breath through their noses and hold it until I say,

"Run," at which point they sprint to the five-, ten-, and fifteen-yard lines, holding their breath as long as they can. Some individuals may be able to maintain a breathless state the whole time, but not everyone. How long they make it for doesn't matter to me. My goal is to simply create a setting where practice feels more challenging than a game and to instill in their bodies a unique internal reaction. There is evidence to support the idea that when we hold our breath, the spleen contracts, releasing a large number of red blood cells into the bloodstream that stays there for a while.[20] This seems like a similar response to elevation training without elevation, in my opinion.

Without having to hike at high altitudes beforehand, nasal breathing and holding our breath at precise points throughout our training session may improve our circulation and help us acclimatize to hunting at greater elevations, such as in Spain for Ibex. Walking up hills is beneficial, but not everyone can access a tall mountain where they can practice. Make your next hike more challenging by nasal breathing and holding your breath occasionally to prepare for the next season.

Roadside advice: have you ever been stalking a wild game and felt like your heart was beating out of your chest? I have, as a fact. When it happens, try taking a deep breath in through the nose with an extremely slow exhale out the nose. This is a great chance to use breathing techniques in a situation that, if you let it, might become overwhelming or, conversely, one in which you feel more at ease, focused, and in control. When you start breathing via your nose instead of your mouth and pay attention to your breathing pattern, you'll notice that your breath has changed from being short and tense to one that feels natural.

Realigning Mental Health

Take ten deep breaths in through your nose, followed by a very slow exhalation out your nose, whenever you begin to feel stress, anxiety, anger, overwhelmed, or depression rising (remember tongue placement) of any degree. Inhaling and exhaling deeply and slowly from the nose can help pull more oxygen from the air and allow us to enter a state of calmness, ease, and inner peace. This can buy you some more time and help you regain yourself. When we breathe through our mouths heavily, our bodies go into a "fight or flight" response, whereas when we breathe through our noses, we feel relaxation inside. You might be shocked by how your breathing mechanics can affect your thoughts and emotions by increasing the amount of oxygen reaching the brain and controlling your heart rate. There will be some fortunate circumstances in life, as well as unfortunate, unfavorable, and even fatal ones. You can better grasp and embrace these situations by being more present with them when you inhale deeply and slowly exhale out of the nose.

If you want to adopt it, nasal breathing is a crucial part of consciousness transformation. In fact, I once conducted an experiment in which I told my sophomore-senior students in a high school class I developed called "human potential" to sit still and be silent for fifteen minutes, focusing only on their surroundings (the classroom). Every time they had a thought that had nothing to do with the classroom, such as what they were going to eat for lunch, that homework assignment they forgot to turn in, weekend plans, and so on, they had to jot it down on a sheet of paper in their notebook before returning to being present. For my class, the range of different thoughts that had nothing to do with the classroom was between fifty and ninety per person.

A few weeks later, we tested the same duration again with my class, but this time, before we began, I told them to concentrate just on nasal breathing, huge breaths in, and slow breaths out the entire time without explaining why. We counted their thoughts after the fifteen-minute session, which had drastically decreased to seven to twenty-two per person. After that lesson, I had many students who had epiphanies about how important breathing patterns are for their mental health. Some students would later share with me how they had included nasal breathing routines before nightfall when they had a plethora of thoughts racing through their heads that made them feel overwhelmed by stress, and they claimed this had worked beautifully—music to my ears.

With more structure, give it a try for yourself. Put your tongue on the roof of your mouth first, then close your mouth. Next, slowly inhale through the nose for five seconds. Hold your breath for five seconds. Finally, gently exhale out your nose for at least five seconds. Imagine breathing in the fresh air with a sense of internal ease while slowly exhaling to let all of your anxious thoughts leave out your nose. Try this several times until you start to feel more relaxed and present.

Potential Benefits of Nasal Breathing:	
Regulate heart rate and blood pressure	Decrease headaches
Improve endurance	Improve proper postural muscles
Improve sleep quality	Filter out bacteria, viruses, and chemicals
Improve energy conservation	
Improve circulation	Control the quantity and quality of your thoughts and emotions
Improve your ability to be patient	
Decrease mood swings	Decrease chronic stress
Decrease depression	Decrease anxiety and panic attacks
Enhanced creativity and self-awareness	Decrease anger
	Find solutions to problems
Improve oral and gut health	Decrease teeth grinding

Let's say you want to know when nasal breathing is a good idea. The answer is to do as much as possible, everywhere, and anytime. I'm not suggesting that you never again breathe through your mouth. I believe at the very least, there are certain situations when nasal breathing can greatly impact you, such as during the hunt, when you're anxious, before bed, stressed out at work, and during training (warm-up, session, cool down). Like firing a rifle, nasal breathing is a skill that can be developed with repetition. We can enter new levels of physical, mental, and spiritual wellness by developing the ability to breathe more easily through our nasal passages, which also increases our chances of experiencing more opening days and hunting opportunities.

STILLNESS

It's likely that life occasionally feels rushed if you live close to a major town or city. Some people love this way of life, while others don't. In any case, it's critical to examine our lives honestly to assess the pace at which we move through them and if they impact our well-being. For this reason, I believe there is an idea worth investigating, particularly if you find yourself living a fast-paced lifestyle that involves multitasking, hurrying around, and giving your attention to everyone and everything. And that is stillness. Stillness, in simple terms, is about breaking the addiction of thought by focusing on being in the present with an absence of movement. You will discover as you get older that where we place our attention matters because our thoughts and emotions can transfer us from the present moment to the past, the future, and our fantasies. The more we allow our attention to wander without control, the more we forget things, become overstimulated, and suddenly feel like our thoughts and emotions are taking up too much space in our minds. As a result, we start to change into someone we are not.

Being present through intense focus and learning how to lessen distracting and useless thoughts are two key components of stillness. It is possible to uncover yourself—your true, innermost self—by engaging in this meditation-like practice, especially when completed in a setting of natural solitude. Consider practicing stillness if you struggle with overthinking to reduce problems that seem overwhelming.

How to start a stillness session:

STEP 1: Remove your phone and place it in a location where you won't be tempted to look at it. Wear a digital watch for timing purposes.

STEP 2: Aim to put yourself in a natural solitude setting (mountains, beaches, lakes, riverbanks, etc.) by yourself. If this cannot be accomplished, aim for a setting with fewer people and environmental distractions.

STEP 3: Sit on the ground or in a chair.

STEP 4: For at least twenty minutes, remain still and silent while nasal breathing. Try your best to think solely about things related to the environment as you concentrate on what is going on around you. The tendency to overthink tends to fade into the background if you give nature your attention, like the snail creeping on a nearby tree limb. If you have a thought that has nothing to do with your surroundings, notice it, examine it, and then go back to your original focus (similar to my classroom experiment).

STEP 5: Keep track of how much time you spend thinking exclusively about your surroundings for a given period of time. Every session, try to increase (extend) your time by continuously practicing.

Think about sitting on the ground near a lake, upright. You are sitting still, silent, alone, eyes open, aware of what is going on in your head regarding the environment. The task is straightforward: by deliberately focusing, try your best to stay in the zone of thoughts relating to your environment. What about that fleeting thought that just crept into your head regarding the electricity bill you need to pay? That thought is not connected to the trees, birds, and water around you.

Potential Benefits of Stillness Practice:	
Decreased chronic stress	Improved memory
Heightened senses	Improved patience
Increased creativity	Improved self-awareness
Enhanced intellectual abilities	Decreased anger
Being more present	Less uneasiness
Improved focus	Inner peace
Better control of our attention	Reduced depression
Reduced anxiety	More happiness

Moving quickly through life and allowing our minds to race around with uncontrollable random thoughts might lead to an emotional roller coaster that can feel out of our hands. We can start to acquire clarity the moment we give our thoughts regarding the surroundings our entire attention. When you realize that you and the thoughts and emotions from your memory and imagination have been the source of how you react to situations in life, you can achieve pure consciousness (totally aware) through stillness practice. To examine our specific problems and seek out the root of our ignorance, we must be able to look within ourselves with real focus. This is what pure consciousness entails. You can find all the answers you've ever wanted in life once you take the time to look into "this" in depth. Once you start practicing stillness, deep within, your energy shifts to the point where those around you can sense this unexplainable energy pouring forth from your body. It is going to be quite contagious.

Location and Silence

The chance to spend time outdoors is a perk that hunters get to have. I believe being in nature can assist us in entering a state where stress and tension can start to reduce, making it one of the better antidepressant and antianxiety remedies available. Use your downtime to practice stillness to gain the potential benefits mentioned earlier when you are on your next hunt, such as when you are in Missouri waiting in a blind for that turkey to appear. Make a point of enjoying nature even when it's not hunting season by visiting places like mountains, beaches, lakes, and riverbanks.

Mother Nature has numerous ways of assisting you in discovering more perspective within yourself and your thoughts once you begin to comprehend that the soil, plants, rocks, air, and water all exist for various reasons. One of those is to bring you back to the present. The background noises throughout your stillness session will be low-grade, peaceful, and calming if you can conduct it in a natural setting with less artificial noise.

Aim for finding a place with fewer people and external distractions if a natural setting during the off-season is not possible for your stillness session. It may be more difficult because the noise level is different and probably greater in an artificial environment, but it is still worthwhile to attempt.

For many people, one of the big challenges of conducting a stillness session is to do it without any external background noise, such as music, TV news, a podcast, or a phone video. This can result from the shortage of silent moments in our lives. Because we build habits such as requiring constant background noise and external stimulation, it's possible that we are slightly allergic to being alone and quiet with our thoughts. This could explain why so many find silence unsettling and say that it disturbs them. Due to the silence that comes with stillness, we are forced to confront our true selves. This is an excellent opportunity to examine the caliber of the thoughts and narratives that dominate our minds.

I'm not advocating that we never listen to music or have the TV or a podcast on. I'm just saying that taking some time to be still and be silent, like during a stillness session, can help us refocus our thoughts and regain accurate self-awareness about what we are doing, and why. Welcome silence with open arms.

Being by Yourself

It can be daunting to complete a stillness session by yourself at first. Nevertheless, the benefits from the individual realizations that may result from it could be life changing. To me, increasing our capacity for experiencing pleasantness within—otherwise known as better mental health—is another step toward actual joy and happiness. It is worthwhile to work on improving the way our minds work because if we incorporate meditation-based practices, we may end up lessening symptoms of anxiety, depression, eating disorders, chronic pain, and substance abuse.[21]

When my father was a martial arts instructor, candidates for a first-degree black belt had to undergo three months of demanding physical and mental testing. The "three-day outdoor requirement" was one of the last tests to get a first-degree black belt. My father would drop off martial arts students in the Oregon coast woods, usually during December when the weather was nasty and cold, to stay by themselves to begin this three-day outdoor experience. The student's goal was to gain perspective, be more present with their thoughts and emotions, practice technique, and acquire a stronger appreciation of nature and oneself while being alone without technology. This idea was inspired by the time when my father spent a few months living in a cave in New Zealand by himself to deepen his connection to nature and improve his martial arts skills.

Now that I think about it, this three-day outdoor requirement was in many ways like stillness. I didn't realize it at the time, being in the truck while my father dropped these students off, that my father knew the transformation these students were about to go through. One of the best teachers we all have access to is nature. Nature teaches us how to accept things completely as they are. In nature, there are no comparisons.

> Being alone in a natural setting with silence gives you the opportunity to relax, slow down, step back from society, be at ease, and recenter yourself.

Alone in nature without technology is a tremendous opportunity to get to know oneself better on the inside and out. Discovering your true self in relation to the environment, the world, and the universe is a unique opportunity for you to transform into a happier person. Perform a stillness session or three-day outdoor seclusion from people and technology to reap the benefits, as what happens physically, mentally, and spiritually may surprise you. Nature is always waiting for you.

My Personal Experience

I've improved greatly at detaching from reactive and emotionally charged thoughts through my own stillness sessions. For me, this has come from countless hours of effort reprogramming my brain's software to respond to circumstances more effectively. Although I am far from flawless, I am improving. I am now progressing toward a very valuable state a human being can experience, self-actualization, by identifying the sources of my ignorance through internal observation.

Even though my stillness practice is tough, I embrace it because it brings me to greater levels of consciousness that I had no idea existed. I've discovered that as I sharpen the quality of my stillness sessions, I become more at ease and aware of my surroundings, and I have greater control over where I can swiftly send my inner energy. This gives me a deeper awareness of who I am from moment to moment, second to second, which is true freedom.

One of the hardest things in life to understand is yourself and your thought quality. However, if a person chooses to look within, they can embark on one of the greatest journeys. Those who try to rewire themselves internally will feel profoundly liberated at the core. If you're ready to venture in, that is.

THE "WILL"

The "will" was another subject I learned when practicing martial arts in my youth. Although I now have a deeper understanding of this powerful spiritual tool as time has passed, it is still difficult to deconstruct. Let's keep things simple. Realize there is a distinction between the "will" and the mind. Your mind tells you that you want those crackers; the "will" says, *Shut up, we don't need those crackers*. After spotting an elk, your mind advises you against hiking up the mountain since it will be too exhausting and too much work. *More work and effort*, according to your "will," are better. You are too cold and wet to go on that solo deer hunt, your mind tells you. *You go* because your "will" acknowledges that being able to hunt is a blessing. All these scenarios are real if you want your "will" to say them.

The mind prefers to choose the path with less difficulty, loves comfort, and longs for pleasure. It constantly seeks out fast gratification, quick results, brief thrills, and shortcuts, like pressing a button. These qualities won't ever provide us with true satisfaction or the results we desire. The "will" is the master, not the mind, and it requires ongoing nurturing to develop into an unstoppable force.

> When used consistently and effectively by an individual, the "will" is a powerful spiritual weapon.

If we want it to, our "will" has the potential to overcome anything in life. In other words, if we aren't taking care of our health but want to make changes in our lives, we can get there with the help of our "will," provided we practice consistent self-discipline. Self-discipline includes things like putting more effort into your significant relationship, working out frequently, cutting back on snacks, etc. All of us can develop these habits; we simply need to indulge less in comfort. Not too much TV or screen time, less couch time, reducing our alcohol consumption, etc. If you choose to indulge in comfort, do so in moderation. However, keep in mind that the more we do so and bask in it, the more stagnant we may become, the less likely it is that we will experience personal growth, the more likely it is that we may regret it, and the more likely it is that we could become distanced from everything we want to achieve in life and while hunting. Maybe think about redefining comfort as something we can earn if we continually practice self-discipline with our lifestyle choices. For instance, if you make time to train, reward yourself by watching your preferred hunting TV program.

If a lot of things in your life aren't going well, start concentrating on strengthening your "will" by making yourself less comfortable, doing what you said you were going to do, keeping your attention on what you can control, taking on new challenges, and actively pursuing your goals. Recognize that we can use our "will" to shape ourselves into the person we want to be and to live the life we want if we consistently do hard things every day.

We must also be conscious that cultivating self-discipline often means doing things we don't particularly want to do. Like choosing to go for a run in spite of the fact that it is pouring rain and extremely cold outside, even if we don't want to. You've strengthened the "will" by exerting greater self-discipline by responding that way. When we consistently adopt and embrace self-discipline, especially during moments when we don't want to do things, it is a factor in life that causes us to feel incredibly proud of ourselves. Let me rephrase that. If you want to be more proud of yourself, instill self-discipline for making better lifestyle choices; you won't regret it, ever.

Since it enables us to handle the ups and downs of life more effectively and promotes inner stability, developing our "will" is one of the most rewarding tasks we can take on. There are moments and situations every day where we can apply greater self-discipline and improve our position in life. Once we realize that the "will" can be strengthened at anytime, we can soon register that our response to even the littlest things can decide what kind of person we become. Like the moment you were tempted to make fun of someone but decided in a split second to restrain yourself from expressing those poor character attributes that your mind thought of. That is a victory for the "will."

Submitting less to the first thought that comes to mind demonstrates that you have a strong "will" and better self-control. You don't have to eat the cookies just because your manager at work brings them in every Friday, and your mind tells you that you ought to.

Believing

The "will" has the power to influence our health—more than merely doing or taking anything. It can drive true positive thinking in the mind and body. For instance, if you were told that taking medication would stop your painful migraines, your positive thinking derived from the "will" that "this medication is going to cure me of these migraines" can actually help you heal yourself even though you weren't aware that the medication solely contained processed sugar. The processed sugar pill does nothing to help with your migraines. But because you strongly believed that the medication would work as promised, your migraines stopped.

There are countless real stories of individuals who have used their "will" to believe they can recover from a minor health condition or even a chronic disease, and despite all the odds, they managed to prevail because of their "will" and beliefs. How does this work?

Our body may self-manufacture the things we need inside for greater health if we innately, with every cell of our being, believe something to heal ourselves or help our health. In this context, it is referred to as the "power of hope" from the "will." Even if there is no assurance of total immunity and every person and circumstance differs, we might be able to improve our situations to some degree with a stronger thought process formed from the "will." What you believe may truly have an impact on how you feel and how your health is doing on some level. This implies that, on the other hand, if your beliefs are negative, they could also negatively affect your health.

Could the "will" govern the mind and body to heal better, age better, and avoid and defeat chronic disease? It's possible. There is reason to believe that practicing self-discipline from the "will" by making better lifestyle choices and believing in or practicing positive thinking could be somewhat helpful. It can be tough to cultivate this optimistic outlook and the belief that you can beat sickness during trying times. If this is the case, you might want to investigate the field of psychoneuroimmunology and the various aspects of hypnotherapy as a tool to assist you and your "will" in believing you can overcome the health limitation, addiction, trauma, chronic disease, and so on.

The Best Gift for Guides and Outfitters

Regarding the clients of guides and outfitters, this is one of the discussions where I think the "will" has to be explored. Both frequently have clients who have overindulged in comfort and under indulged in the necessary planning and preparation for the hunt. If you utilize guides or outfitters, in my opinion, make sure to prepare your "will" in advance. By doing this, you are placing yourself in a position to have the internal support system needed to be mentally tough when faced with adversity on your hunt.

If you have a stronger "will," you will go the extra distance necessary to locate the pursued wild game, regardless of the discomfort. Even though you are physically fatigued, having a strong "will" is evident when you ask your guide and outfitter how you can assist in breaking down the enormous bull moose.

Consistent training before your trip can help you develop a fine-tuned "will" and lessen any physical limitations you could experience while hunting. Gaining strength and physical fitness may increase your confidence in handling the trip's physical demands.

Hunting is more enjoyable for you when you are physically and mentally prepared, and it is also more enjoyable for the guides and outfitters who are helping you. The guide or outfitter does not need to be treated like a butler, housekeeper, or servant. I think we should treat them like we would a close friend or part of our family. Find moments to assist them during the trip. Assist them with tasks such as setting up the wall tent, doing the dishes, gathering water, cutting firewood, loading the horses, mules, and llamas, breaking down the wild game, and packing the meat out. No matter how much wild game we see or whether we are successful, take these actions. I'd wager to assume that guides and outfitters would appreciate clients who are more physically and mentally prepared and who are appreciative of their assistance in even the most minor situations. Be that client.

Mentally Tough Hunts

Think back to some of the hunts you've been on in the past when you had thoughts that suggested it wasn't fun, that it was a waste of time because there wasn't any game, or that there were 109 things that went wrong. We've all undoubtedly had similar thoughts at some point in our hunting careers, including myself. The goal is to figure out how to mentally rewire yourself so that when things aren't going well, you can still successfully navigate these hunts. It's about improving as a person and a hunter, not about being flawless.

The truth is as such. On our hunts, there will inevitably be ups and downs. This will happen. More so for some people. It might be the weather, the terrain, faulty equipment, a lack of wild game, etc. No matter if it's an over-the-counter hunt or one we've been applying for that took twenty-two years to get, our mind wants to complain, bicker, and look for any excuse during the hunt to rationalize that the trip is a failure. The "will" is different. In these situations that don't seem to be to our advantage, it responds well. It reacts by internalizing the circumstance and analyzing several aspects of life to put the hunt in perspective. How? Read on.

When things seem dim and gloomy while on the hunt, the "will" uses specific narratives to reflect on. Things like:

1. **Next generation of hunters.** The "will" imagines what kind of role model the next generation of hunters needs. They need an individual who constantly learns and betters themselves in dealing with adversity while on the hunt and in everyday life. Be that someone and show them it's possible to overcome obstacles.
2. **Veterans.** The "will" thinks about the sacrifices veterans have made for us to have the opportunity to hunt. Imagine for a second what veterans on active duty have gone through. Okay, now times that by one hundredfold for what they actually went through. God bless those individuals.

3. **Is it that bad?** The "will" says it's not. What is bad is the thousands of children who are abducted from their families, terrified to death, and then sold to human traffickers worldwide. Or the thousands of children who are diagnosed with chronic, life-threatening diseases and must deal with pain, discomfort, and treatment every day before they even get a chance to live. Our hunt is not bad.
4. **One in 400 trillion.** The "will" understands that these are the rough odds and chances of being born and having a life.[22] Basically, your chances of witnessing an alien and a sasquatch riding a unicorn up a mountain are better than your chances of ever having a life. Make the most of all you can because this life goes by quickly as we are truly a miracle.

Be persistent and patient; it takes time to fully surrender and set aside our ego to really adopt these narratives. Strive to be conscious of them and thoroughly internalize them by reflecting on your life in relation to them to become aware of how blessed you are to have the ability to hunt. Maybe before your next hunt, pick one and write it down somewhere visible—on your bow, rifle, shotgun, in a tiny notepad, as the background of your phone, etc.—so that you can see it while out in the field. Internally reprogramming yourself is worthwhile, as you'll realize it's a win-win no matter what happens during your hunt. That's how I currently feel, at least.

My brother and I on an archery elk hunt.

With this image, several thoughts spring to mind. This was the first time I realized how much I valued a pack with a sturdy design that could support hefty loads. I was using a pack at the time that was incapable of supporting the weight and providing the maneuverability I required for this backcountry trip. I had an elk quarter in it that was poorly built and it made my lower back bleed. In the end, my brother's buddy let me borrow his Kifaru pack (as seen in the photo), which was significantly different from my pack at the time in that it made the load feel weightless and comfy due to its efficient design. Soon after this trip, I purchased a Kifaru pack, which I still use today because of how it performs and feels.

On this trip, I began to reflect on my connection to nature. It seemed like I finally grasped how alluring the outdoors are to me—not because of the hunt itself, but just by being there. The environment of nature is like a magnet that is always attempting to draw us in for reasons we may never understand.

GROUNDING

Hunting exposes us to many of the remarkable characteristics of the natural world. The very thing we think is pulling us in (the pursuit of wild game) to some degree could be our cells reinforcing to our body, mind, and spirit how badly they want to be in a natural environment. The fact that the earth has healing properties is one of the underlying reasons why our being is drawn to these natural settings. The earth can improve our health in a variety of ways. I feel like one of them is significantly underrated. And that is grounding, which some people refer to as "earthing."

Grounding is accomplished by having our skin come into contact with the earth's surface, such as grass, soil, sand, riverbanks, gardens, and lakeshores. For instance, we can accomplish this by being barefoot on our backyard's dirt. When we are barefoot on the earth's surface, we start to absorb electrons (a transfer of energy) from the earth's core. These electrons act as antioxidants and anti-inflammatories in our bodies. In essence, grounding is a chance for the earth to heal and rejuvenate us in terms of improving our physical, mental, and spiritual well-being.

The effectiveness of grounding depends on how consistent we are and our current health status. Results could come quickly, moderately, or slowly. It is a strategy, if applied consistently, can improve our health on various levels. It is not necessarily something we do only once to be healed and well. The more we spend time grounded, the more vitality we might feel. Aim for at least thirty minutes for each session each day as a general guideline.

Grounding may have a positive impact on wound healing, prevention and treatment of autoimmune and chronic diseases, and a reduction in inflammation.[23] Additionally, it has been shown that grounding could possibly lower the risk of cardiovascular disease by reducing the clumping of red blood cells in our bodies.[24] Additionally, it might aid in decreasing pain, enhancing mood, and improving sleep.[25]

For hunters, a fantastic opportunity to get grounding in while on the hunt could be in camp, depending on the terrain and environment. Consider going barefoot if you can while in camp or even taking a break from the pursuit, especially if you are out hunting with a headache, stomachache, or simply feeling generally unwell. This may be an opportunity for the earth to heal you.

Conditions and Processes *Potentially* Improved by Consistent Grounding:		
Arthritis	PTSD	Hormones
Eczema	Migraines and headaches	Gut health
Anxiety		Hives
Depression	Focus and memory	Skin burns
Fast/irregular heartbeats	Surgery	Busy mind
Sleep quality	Hot Flashes	Infertility
Glaucoma	Plantar Fasciitis	Muscle soreness
Varicose veins	Vertigo	

When used consistently, grounding nearly seems to have an infinite number of health benefits that it could be able to provide, such as happiness, a better moral compass, increased energy, and faster recovery when you have a physical injury. However, it is essential to discuss with your primary doctor if grounding is appropriate for you if you are taking any prescription medications for its impact. For instance, grounding is a natural blood thinner, so if you take pharmaceutical blood thinners, the dosage may need to be changed.

You can take advantage of this amazing health-promoting component the earth has to give by grounding in your yard, when shooting your bow, while camping, etc.

Suppose that we are unable to make direct contact with the ground. In such a situation, many people benefit from the grounding products that are now available online, such as sleeping pads, pillowcases, and work mats for the feet and forearms that we can plug into a building outlet (assuming it is a grounded outlet). In principle, the earth's electrons move from the grounded outlet to the pad, simulating what happens when one has direct skin contact with the earth.

When I had poison oak two years ago, I used grounding sessions. Because of my severe allergy to poison oak, I frequently needed a shot or prescription medication to get rid of it. This time, after six days of daily, thirty-minute grounding sessions in my backyard, my poison oak receded and completely vanished. Whether it was from grounding or the result of my "will," the poison oak disappeared in about a week instead of the usual month. When we consider what grounding may accomplish for the body, the fact that wild game are constantly grounded may be the reason why they heal from injuries so quickly.

Healthy Feet

Beyond grounding sessions, there are further advantages of being barefoot. Let me set the scene for you. Humans used to run and walk barefoot many years ago. Then, as time passed, we created and used thin-soled running and walking shoes with little cushioning and support. Today, we have shoes that offer a ton of padding for protection and cushioning for our feet. The most important thing to take away from this timeline is that we are moving in a direction where we are gradually shielding our feet from the outside world. Is this pattern beneficial to our health? Possibly not.

It's usually a good idea to wear boots or other types of footwear in cold or rugged terrain to reduce pain and the risk of damage from potentially sharp objects while hunting. It seems sensible to wear shoes in these circumstances. However, it might not be optimal for us to spend most of the day in shoes, especially in the off-season, and spend very little time barefoot. When we begin to analyze the people who are walking and running in less-developed countries, we find something interesting; they are often barefoot or with minimal footwear. These people also tend to have fewer physical injuries/pain (knee, back, hips) than more developed countries that wear the most advantaged types of shoes.[26] Why is that so? It might be because of the way our feet were designed.

Our feet were built to use the muscles around them to stabilize the ankles, knees, hips, and spine while maintaining balance by using the toes to grab the ground. The foundation of our entire physical structure is our feet. When we put on shoes, the base of our movement is modified to suit the shoe's design, making it more unnatural (artificial). Placing our feet in compromised positions, shoes with raised heels, extra gel cushioning, modified arches, and curved shapes over time may harm our ligaments, joints, bones, and posture. The less time we spend barefoot, the more symptoms we might experience throughout the body, including tightness in the low back, knee, ankle, and foot problems, bunions and weak feet, tendon stiffness, plantar fasciitis, and muscle strains. Being more barefoot may, in certain cases, help avoid and correct these imbalances.

Watch the feet of a one-year-old child beginning to walk if you need an example of how the feet function more efficiently while they are barefoot. To increase stability, their toes tighten and shift all the time. If we were to put shoes on them while they were learning to walk, it would take them a lot longer to learn and would also potentially change how they would walk in the future.

I'm not advocating that we never put on shoes again. It's pretty comfortable to wear boots when hunting those high-country Mule deer up a steep, rocky mountain. I'm simply suggesting we actively look for moments to go barefoot to realign our bodies. My favorite places to go barefoot are at home, on the beach, in parks with wet grass, and at hunting camps. Make an extra effort to find occasions like those I've mentioned where you can go barefoot; I'm confident you can. The more barefoot activities we engage in, especially outside, the better it is for our bones, muscles, and bodies over time.

GARDENING

While keeping the mindset of all the benefits of being outside, gardening comes to mind. The ability to develop a garden, not only as a source of food but also to gain perspective on life, is one of the most unappreciated yet valuable skills to have. We can develop a stronger connection to the cycles of life by gardening. We can learn to enjoy the beginning of a plant's life, how it lives, and how it dies by growing flowers, fruits, vegetables, or herbs. By realizing how quickly time passes, we can become more grateful for our lives by appreciating the beauty of life's cycles.

My mother has been tending to her garden for a long time. She grows fruits and vegetables in superior quality soil than at the industrial level; thus, they are unmatched in terms of nutrient quality (vitamin and mineral content). Industrial-level agriculture (monocrop) uses tilling and spraying pesticides and highly deadly chemicals that destroy the beneficial bacteria that are supposed to help maintain the soil's health and nutrient-rich status. The same holds true for organic produce. Because pesticides are still used on organic crops, these soil bacteria suffer. Produce labeled "organic" does not always guarantee greater health.

A large number of living things, like bees, reptiles, and rodents that were living on the land, could also be harmed by industrial-level agriculture by threatening their habitats and sources of food.[27] But having our own garden prevents these negatives from occurring.

Produce grown in gardens is more nutrient-dense and may be able to absorb carbon emissions due to better soil quality. To combat climate change, I have seen many people begin to convert their front or backyard into a small produce area. Visit the Save Soil campaign of Conscious Planet for further details on the importance of healthy soil on a global basis.

At the absolute least, we can get our hands dirty with nonconsumable plants like flowers if growing fruits, veggies, or herbs does not sound enticing. I don't know about you, but whenever I see a flower bloom, it immediately makes me joyful with far more "good energy." There is evidence that gardening can improve life satisfaction and reduce anxiety and depression.[28] By growing our own food, we may also be able to lower our shopping bills, improve gut health and boost our immune system (thanks to touching the healthy soil bacteria), and get more fresh air and sunlight. Even having exposure to outdoor pets and or farm animals who spend time in and around healthy soil (dirt) can improve our health on a variety of levels. On your next hunting trip, get your hands dirty; healthy soil is king.

Gardening could also promote brain health, which can help with thinking abilities.[29] We can unwind, become more conscious, and appreciate life to a greater extent when we have plants to water. It's probably reasonable to say that when hunters fully commit to this activity, they might experience perks.

ANIONS

You may have wondered, *Why do I feel so good when I am out in nature?* when out hunting. Anions may very well be one of those factors. Anions, also known as negative ions, are airborne molecules that are tasteless, odorless, invisible, and carry extra oxygen. They are common in natural settings such as mountains, waterfalls, forests, beaches, and rivers. These kinds of natural settings are full of anions, which help us oxygenate and circulate our bodies better. Hence, when you take a deep breath in close to a waterfall, you feel incredibly alive inside!

Since the air near trees is the epitome of a healthy atmosphere, my preferred location to acquire anions is up in the mountains surrounded by timber. To a certain extent, trees can purify and filter the air around them by capturing airborne pollutants, just like air filters do. Try to spend as much time as possible near trees because their pure air and anions can enter our bloodstream and possibly cause beneficial effects in our bodies, such as elevating our mood and reducing anxiety and chronic stress, particularly when we breathe in through our noses. Doesn't that sound better than the toxic air we frequently breathe in buildings?

The key is to spend time outside in these wooded, natural settings outside of hunting season. In these natural settings, consider walking your pet, shooting your bow/rifle, practicing stillness, hiking with the family, reading books, scouting, cultivating art, going camping, writing, shed hunting, and so on. Immerse yourself in the healthy and filtered air, natural light exposure, and unquestionable health benefits an individual can experience by being around anions, trees, and nature.

MODIFY YOUR ENVIRONMENT

Let's address an issue that is being ignored: the toxins in indoor air that we frequently breathe in buildings. But first, get a load of this.

A typical adult spends 87 percent of their time indoors and 6 percent in enclosed vehicles, according to a study by the Environmental Protection Agency.[30] If you multiply this by a typical workweek of Monday through Friday for thirty years, you will find that there is very little time that an adult might very well spend outdoors.

Imagine yourself in a situation where, aside from when you go hunting, you spend most of your time indoors. In that case, it might be wise to consider, if possible, incorporating plants into the buildings you are in. Bring some nature into your building since it can benefit your health. The volatile organic compounds (VOCs) found in building materials, air fresheners, cosmetics, and cleaning products, among others, have been shown to cause everything from minor headaches (short-term exposure) to more serious health problems, like kidney and liver damage, from long-term exposure.[31] Indoor potted plants, however, may be able to remove a significant amount of the VOCs that get produced in an indoor environment.[32]

When I think of VOCs I think of artificial scents and fragrances put into products (detergent, hair spray, soap, perfume, cologne, cosmetics, shampoo, dryer sheets, deodorant, etc.) that are featured all over TV ads as being very refreshing. They may be refreshing to some, but they also potentially upset our hormones when we breathe them in or wear them on a continuous basis. As I mentioned in the dietary section, look at the *ingredients* of these products. Look them up online. You might be surprised by the effects of using some of these products and ingredients on our bodies and minds over time. Make an effort to learn about the products you use, such as the ones listed, and look for better alternatives if possible. You may recall that one of the advantages mentioned in the section on nasal breathing was the ability to filter out chemicals. The next time you are surrounded by synthetic scents and fragrances, keep that in mind.

Inflammation is one of the first steps in developing many diseases, and VOCs can also trigger it within the body. Consider purchasing an air purifier to help detoxify the indoor air in your home from these products, in addition to adding plants. If you frequently travel a long distance for work, consider keeping a window open to let fresh air in.

OUR INTERNAL WATER

Water is essential to this world on many levels, including our need to consume it, the need for it to serve as a home for many species, the need for it to be used in manufacturing, and so on. However, it is interesting to notice that humans are mainly comprised of water throughout their bodies. In a way, we are like water bottles.

And since we are literally water bottles, the conversation with water and its environment gets interesting when we begin to realize that the water throughout our body can change its structure based on our response to the frequencies (sounds/words) of the surrounding environment. The sounds we are around, along with the quality of words verbally expressed (positive or negative), change the water's frequency vibration (altering the water molecular structure) inside of us. Depending on how we react to them, they may place our body in a healthy state or an unhealthy state.

Where do you think your body should be to receive the frequency vibrations from healthy sounds? The outdoors and our hunt are one location. For our body's internal water to react favorably, a more natural state of noise is required from birds, wind, trees, wild game calls, bugs, and so on. With this lifestyle, I believe we can cross that off the list.

Since the sounds (music, news, etc.) we are exposed to can affect our internal state, it is important to pay great attention and reflect on our surroundings during the off-season if we feel we are having a bad day. Be conscious of the fact that the type of sounds we expose to our body can affect our mood, behavior, emotions, and mental health. Look into the sounds you are exposing to your ears from your phone, computer, and TV if you are experiencing a day where certain traits are hindered. Choose sounds that are more uplifting, inspiring, and positive. One song on your favorite playlist that gives you these feelings can actually alter your course in life.

Think about the people you surround yourself with. There is a reason why you like to be around particular hunting partners. Some claim that we start to adopt many of the personality traits of the people we spend a lot of time with. Depending on the person's character, this may be beneficial or negative. Think for a moment. Imagine spending a few months surrounded by people who mostly expressed words related to humility, optimism, honesty, hard work, drive, kindness, and so forth. My guess is that our demeanor and well-being could change somewhat for the better.

It's crucial to realize how powerful positive words from those we are in close proximity to can affect our internal health and well-being. There is no doubt a greater risk of developing bad internal health if we are surrounded by people or even just one person who frequently complains, bickers, is egotistical, gossips about others, is pessimistic, has a poor moral compass, etc. If we spend enough time around these people, our attitudes, thoughts, and emotions may change badly, regardless of our awareness of them.

Aim to speak and express yourself positively to other people so that their internal waters can be healthier due to the words' frequency vibrations. Be the change that is needed in someone else's life. Their water may respond well and so may yours. Your water's positive response to particular frequencies (sounds/words) from the environment can help your body and mind become healthy. Adhere to the outdoors and uplifting people as much as possible.

THE SUN

There has always been a big, glowing object in the sky that we call the sun. Depending on where you are in the world, your exposure to it may vary. It's crucial to realize how important this enormous shining object is to our health and well-being, no matter where you are. By boosting our energy levels, improving our mental health, strengthening our immune system, and doing many other things to keep us healthy, natural sunlight gives us an opportunity to revitalize our body, mind, and spirit. Some folks may feel scared of the sun. When we start to consider what it can do for our physical, mental, and spiritual health when obtaining a proper amount of exposure, it appears to offer many benefits.

One of those wonderful powers is providing us with naturally occurring vitamin D. Direct sunlight reacts with our skin to synthesize vitamin D and convert it to vitamin D3, which produces various health effects within us. This vitamin, also known as a hormone, is crucial for human health for many practical reasons, one of which is that it regulates a wide range of genes.[33] When you hear "regulate genes," it typically means that they can either turn on (express themselves) or turn off (not express themselves). Having sufficient vitamin D levels may:[34]

- Improve memory
- Balance hormones
- Keep teeth and bones strong
- Decrease anxiety
- Decrease aggression
- Regulate blood pressure
- Improve mood
- Decrease depression
- Improve autoimmune conditions
- Improve gut health
- Promote better quality sleep

We have been told that exposure to the sun has negative health effects, which is one of the main reasons people try to avoid it. Without a doubt, prolonged sun exposure that results in frequent sunburns harms our health in the long run. However, moderate sun exposure can have a tremendous positive impact on our health. The key to avoiding sunburns is to increase our sun exposure gradually. Try to spend five to sixty minutes in the sun, depending on your skin tone. Be self-aware of how certain time frames should be adjusted for your particular needs based on elevation, location, age, and time of day.

There are several foods we can eat that contain vitamin D3 if, for whatever reason, it is difficult to get enough sunlight. Some of the better sources are animal-based, including wild game, grass-fed meat, wild-caught fatty fish or cod liver oil, and egg yolks from pasture-raised chickens. Since I reside in Oregon, I make sure to eat a fair amount of these foods to meet my needs.

Sunscreen is another topic worth talking about in relation to sunshine. We can reduce the amount of sunscreen we use by giving our skin time to acclimatize to the sunlight and by eating the animal-based foods I mentioned. This is a good thing because many popular sunscreens frequently contain chemicals that when used regularly and broken down by the sun and absorbed by our skin, could seriously harm our health.[35] The tremendous health benefits I stated before are potentially reduced due to sunscreen use since it might prevent vitamin D absorption. Less vitamin D absorption could explain why there is an increased risk of developing skin cancer in less sunny regions.[36]

Aim for layering up with light-colored clothing and hats if your exposure to the sun is regular and out of your control due to your job, sport, location, etc. Additionally, if sunscreen is the only option for whatever reason, look for sunscreens that are suitable for your health that contains mineral-based ingredients. Some people may also need to think about taking a supplemental form of vitamin D3, depending on their location on the planet and access to specific foods. In that case, it is a smart move to consult your primary doctor to establish the appropriate dosage depending on your unique needs.

SAUNA

For a variety of reasons, sauna use has been common in numerous cultures for hundreds of thousands of years. The use of saunas has recently become more widespread across the globe due to the numerous health benefits they provide. In my opinion, saunas are not only beneficial to our health but also a great way to get our bodies ready for hunting in warmer climates.

Assume you are a Rocky Mountain elk hunter in New Mexico. The sun is following your every move, and sweat is pouring down as you walk around with a pack holding your gear and a bow in your hand. If you are not accustomed to the heat, a hunt like this could inhibit your physical and mental performance. It could be more challenging to adequately hydrate with water and electrolytes if we are not used to the heat. Our capacity to focus and concentrate could also be hampered. As a result, our muscles and mind may begin to feel weak and tired. This is a prime example of how regularly using a sauna during the off-season to acclimate yourself may be a great way to get ready for a hunt where you know the weather will probably be warmer.

Cardiovascular disease is quite common in society, so it may be important to know that sauna use can improve cardiovascular functioning.[37] To put it another way, by regularly using a sauna, we might be able to reduce our risk of sudden cardiac death (SCD), fatal coronary heart disease (CHD), and fatal cardiovascular disease (CVD).[38] This is because our cardiovascular system gets blood to our heart and tissues more efficiently. One person dies from a stroke in the United States every three and a half minutes.[39] Interestingly, recent research suggests that regular sauna users may be able to lower their risk of having a stroke.[40]

In terms of muscles, frequent sauna use may be able to reduce muscular atrophy (a process of losing muscle) by increasing the growth hormone.[41] For those who spend a lot of time sitting, have physical limitations or are healing from an injury, this is important. Since sitting reduces movement, the more we sit, the more quickly our muscles may atrophy. But if we regularly use a sauna, we might be able to maintain more muscle, enabling us to continue engaging in the physically demanding activities of hunting trips and daily activities in general.

Potential Benefits of Consistent Sauna Use:[42]	
Elevated immune system functioning	Decreased anxiety and depression
Enhanced learning abilities	Reduced headaches
Improved blood pressure	Faster recovery from the flu
Better focus	Improved arthritis
Improved mood	Enhanced memory
Increased endurance	Preserves muscles

Start at a temperature that feels manageable to you to begin your sauna session. Depending on the type of sauna and humidity levels, for many, starting at about 120 degrees for fifteen to thirty minutes a few times each week is a good option. A general rule of thumb is to gradually increase the temperature once your body adjusts to the heat and eventually aim for a temperature of between 180 and 220 degrees for fifteen to thirty minutes to experience many of the health advantages outlined. Nevertheless, exercise caution and refrain from using the sauna when consuming alcohol or caffeine before, during, or after your sauna session. Always drink plenty of water (preferably filtered) with unrefined salt before and after a session to stay adequately hydrated. In the end, I highly suggest you discuss sauna use with a qualified doctor if you have a medical condition, take prescription drugs, or have any questions regarding your particular needs or the needs of a family member.

COLD EXPOSURE

Depending on what time of year and location we are hunting, exposure to the cold may be an expected encounter. In my opinion, we need to look for opportunities to improve our ability to handle the cold to better prepare for our hunts, similar to how we handle the heat. Simple examples include taking a quick stroll in the cold or reading a book outside without a coat. Both are excellent chances to become more acclimated and comfortable with the cold.

When I was a child, my father encouraged me to leave the window open in my bedroom to become used to the weather, regardless of the temperature. He also taught me how to welcome rain by facing it without much clothing, especially when hauling rocks or cutting firewood. Upon reflection, I can say that these experiences helped me build the mental fortitude necessary to hunt in various weather conditions and better face adversity in life. Try to place yourself in similar situations and temperatures during the off-season if you find yourself hunting in cooler conditions, such as rain, low temperatures, snow, and so on, so your body can adapt before your hunt. Aim to get colder more regularly, but not to the point of hypothermia or frostbite.

Another reason to intentionally seek out cold settings is for the potential health benefits we can obtain. Cold-water immersion is one method of cold exposure that I find interesting. When you take a cold shower or lay in a tub of cold water (perhaps with some ice added), you are engaging in cold-water immersion. Either choice can offer us a wide range of health benefits.

Potential health benefits include:

- Improved immune system strength
- Boosted mental health
- Weight loss
- Improved sleep quality
- Improved mental fortitude
- Balanced hormones

For me, that second benefit is particularly relevant. Last year, a close mentor of mine who was suffering from post-traumatic stress disorder (PTSD) due to his service in Vietnam passed away. He was one of the people who encouraged me to write this book. It took me some time to write those last few sentences.

For those with PTSD, reaching out to a professional and finding out new ways to boost mental health is vital. In fact, from the standpoint of brain health, individuals with PTSD—often referred to as an invisible wound that affects millions of people worldwide—may benefit from cold-water immersion.[43] PTSD can result from abuse, gun violence, assault, medical, combat, and other situations. Afterward, any of those circumstances may lead to symptoms like sleeplessness, depression, aggression, anxiety, suicidal ideation, and so forth. Numerous people with the condition have reported dramatic benefits from regular cold-water immersion sessions, including improved mood, lower stress, better focus, and a sense of being more alive and present. These benefits result from improved hormone balance and increased blood flow to the brain (post-session). Try to include or encourage daily cold-water immersion in a tub or shower in addition to the health-promoting strategies suggested in this book if you or someone you love is dealing with PTSD. There are things you can do to improve your current position; please stay strong.

How to start a cold-water immersion session: If you have control over the water temperature, like in a bathtub, start with a manageable temperature like seventy-five or seventy degrees, and then, with each session, make it colder until you get to the range of forty to fifty-five degrees to experience many of the listed health benefits. Our bodies can adapt to tolerate the stimulus by gradually lowering the water's temperature. Start by entering slowly and with your feet first. To keep your heart rate under control, breathe slowly through your nose before, during, and after entering. Much like when using a sauna, exercise caution and avoid consuming alcohol or caffeine before, during, or after your cold-water immersion session. Discuss cold-water immersion use with a qualified doctor if you have a medical condition, take prescription drugs, or have any questions regarding your particular needs or the needs of a family member. For well-designed cold-water immersion tubs that don't require ice, filter the water, and have a built-in temperature gauge to set the water to the precise temperature you want, check out Plunge, a maker of cold-plunge tubs.

If you don't have the ability to immerse yourself in a cold tub, think about making the last few minutes of your shower cold. I believe that cold showers are grossly underrated. They are quite good at pulling you out of a slump, decreasing laziness, and boosting mental clarity, in addition to improving your health. If some things in life are not going well for any reason, take a shower and make the last few minutes cold. As cold as you can handle. Until things start to improve for you, keep taking cold showers every day. It won't take long.

Once we are more acclimated to the cold water, we can progress to jumping in a lake, pond, river, or ocean. I had the good fortune to participate in a yearly polar plunge that my father organized at one of the beaches in my hometown while I was between the ages of eight and fourteen. The Pacific Ocean on the Oregon coast does not hold back in giving you a chilly welcome.

Immersing oneself in cold water is a great way to get ready for chilly hunting expeditions like those for Marco Polo Sheep in

Tajikistan. Like the times when it's so cold outside that your face feels numb and your nose mucous has frozen or when your fingers and hands feel like paddles. If we undergo cold-water immersion during the off-season, our body may adapt beforehand by not getting as cold while hunting. This is because our body can become more acclimated to the cold environment, no matter if the coldness comes from the winds, snow, or higher elevations.

Ways #41–51 to Age Better and Prevent Disease

41. Incorporate nasal breathing before/during/after training, while hunting, before you sleep, when you want to recenter yourself, etc.
42. Incorporate more stillness (daily/weekly/monthly) in natural settings.
43. Build up your "will" by being more self-disciplined.
44. Practice grounding (direct skin contact with soil, sand, grass, etc.).
45. Get your gardening on.
46. Immerse yourself in nature and to more anions (rivers, forests, waterfalls, mountains, oceans, etc.).
47. Obtain more sunlight exposure in doses according to your skin tone.
48. Modify your environment by bringing plants into your residence and/or work.

49. Surround your water with positive sounds and words.

50. Incorporate sauna use.

51. Incorporate cold-water immersion.

CHAPTER 6

REWIRING OUR BRAIN

Stay a Student and Live Simply

Imagine going back in time to the first hunt you ever went on. Maybe your parents or a friend took you, or perhaps you decided to go on your own without anyone's advice or assistance. Now, take a moment to recall each instance of the hunt's events. There were probably moments when you learned how to do something better or how not to do it. Perhaps you were impatient, moved too quickly, or hurried a shot. All of these are occasionally encountered, even by experienced hunters. The key, as we get older, is to learn from our past mistakes and do our best to avoid making them in the future.

You've probably already embraced the concept of improving your skills and learning from mistakes to some extent. After years of hunts, you have improved your e-scouting, aim, use of terrain for stalks, placement of your tree stand on a trail regularly traveled by game, glassing of open country, patience, and other skills. You started out making simple mistakes, but now you've raised the bar and elevated your game.

The question is if it would be advantageous to apply this same willingness to learn and want to become better hunters in our regular lives and health during the off-season. I'm here to say that it would be worthwhile, absolutely. Why? It is connected to the health of our brains.

It's crucial to understand the importance of maintaining brain health as we age. Our ability to communicate, recall hunting tactics, feel content, control our emotions, be determined to climb that tall mountain searching for Red Stag in New Zealand, and perform other tasks is significantly influenced by the health of our brains. I prefer to compare the human brain to the muscles of the body. Our muscles are stimulated by movement, which is essential for their health. To thrive, our brains need to continue learning. If a person is always learning, making discoveries on a daily basis, reflecting on themselves and their lives, and seeking out ways to maintain brain health as they age, they are considered to be a *student for life*.

Consider how often adults emphasize to the next generation the importance of learning. Don't you agree that adults should practice what they promote and serve as positive role models by doing what they say? I say yes. By using online resources, books, podcasts, seminars, school, and other means, you can educate yourself to help keep a healthy brain. Learning can lead to personal growth and development at any age.

Start by asking yourself how you can improve every aspect of your life. *How can I improve my hunting skills?* as well as *How can I be a better spouse?* or *How do I become healthier?* After that, start by learning how to do it and continue learning. Once we shift gears and start to invest effort into learning, we may find it liberating to constantly and forever be in a state of continuous inquiry. We can always improve and progress in all areas of life if we so want.

When we stop learning, we start to feel older, become stagnant, experience tunnel vision, and are more likely to make snap judgments. Drawing quick conclusions can lead to a stronger sense of control over what we already know and deter us from learning new things, depending on the circumstance. I commonly hear people conclude that "I will never be good at shooting my bow" or "I have tried everything; I cannot lose this additional weight." The process of forming a strong opinion can make us feel less alive and healthy. It is comparable to a closed door where there is no way to see what is on the other side.

By continually learning, we can develop more clarity. Gaining clarity enables us to recognize things for what they are as they change over time. Since everything is constantly changing, what "is" may be more significant than the notion of what "should be." When our mind is not concerned with always being correct or having the most knowledge, we are said to be in a state of clarity.

With clarity, our focus is to go past the information. This gives us the opportunity to better understand the nature of the mind and life. Seeing our own life through the lens of clarity allows us to gain a deeper understanding of our own thought patterns, feelings, emotions, and the root causes of our ignorance. Things about your life start to make sense once you have clarity.

To ensure that we maintain brain health and develop clarity during the off-season and in life in general, there are numerous methods to help you start along the path of becoming a *student for life*. Reading books is one of my particular favorites, so let's start there.

BOOKS

Physical books, in my opinion, are a wonderful gift to humanity. They are portable so that we can take them anywhere, and they also can outlive their creator. One of the reasons I decided to publish my work as a book is so that even after I have moved on to the next stage in life, I can still potentially help hunters experience more opening days and hunting opportunities.

Reading books is a proven way to stimulate brain regions linked to language and intellectual ability. Even when we are not completely aware of it, our vocabulary instantly expands on a number of levels simply by exposure to new words. Reading books can potentially help us get better at preserving our memory, reasoning, problem-solving, thinking, comprehension of concepts, and learning new information—all of which are important aspects of hunting. This may be linked to the idea that people who read books for an average of thirty minutes a day may outlive others who don't read because reading helps preserve cognitive abilities.[44] By improving cognitive abilities (brain functioning), such as by reading, the risk of age-related brain problems might be reduced.

First thing in the morning, during meals, right before bed, weekends, and at hunting camp are a few examples of when I prefer to schedule some reading. Personally, I prefer reading physical books over other formats. Reading physical books may be able to assist us in sharpening our visual focus, which could boost our ability to spot wild game. Online book reading is not necessarily bad, but too much screen time may interfere with our ability to go to sleep and produce enough melatonin.[45] The goal is to avoid overusing artificial screens, so make an effort to occasionally freshen things up by reading physical books or listening to audiobooks.

The key to cultivating the habit of reading is to find the right book(s). You simply need to start looking for topics related to hunting that actually interest you. *The Education of a Bear Hunter* by Ralph Flowers is one of my favorite hunting-related books that I was given as a young child. This novel depicts Ralph's passion for hunting bruins in the Pacific Northwest. I've read that book many times, and each time I do, I get more enjoyment from it.

When looking for book topics other than those associated with hunting, books that inspire the reader are a terrific choice. Once you find a book that genuinely interests you, it may be difficult for you to set it down. I continue to firmly believe that reading books has had a significant positive impact on my thinking, intelligence, and theory of mind. I believe that reading has given me a big creative force that is blooming within me.

> Each page of a book that we read is just like peering over the next ridge looking for deer. Something that completely changes our life could be waiting for us on the other side.

One of my favorite things about reading books is this idea: despite being exposed to more information, the more we read and learn, the less we know. When we discover how little we actually know in the big picture, self-education by reading books can help transform us into a person full of humility—which is a great thing. Every subject is constantly changing and expanding; therefore, I wish I had ten lifetimes to learn all I want to. It's important to understand that even after studying physics for eighty years, I would still not fully know everything about it.

CHESS

When using a bow or rifle to shoot at a target or wild game, many hunters, including myself, might occasionally become overly anxious (rush). Hunters are advised to practice patience as a means of reducing rushing. But what precisely is patience? The ability to accept reality and the fortitude to wait calmly for better moments could be considered traits of patience.[46]

If we can relax and let our bow and rifle accomplish what we want without forcing it, we have patience. When we lack patience, it makes it more likely that outside circumstances could anxiously shape us. Playing chess is one method for improving our lack of patience. In fact, chess is an excellent tool that can help us better manage our emotions during long grocery store lines or slow traffic.

Chess is a meticulous yet beautiful game that when played frequently can help us become more patient. It's a good opportunity to practice strategy, slow-paced movement, calculation, and critical thinking. All of these are skills that can be used in hunting and help us become better hunters.

I believe one of the best places to play chess is at a hunting camp. Particularly if you are hunting in a location where the weather is not ideal, and you must seek refuge in your tent, trailer, or cabin. Play a few chess games if you have to stay inside due to unfavorable weather to keep your mind sharp. It can preserve our brain functioning so we can resume our hunt alert, ready, and patient.

Playing chess not only helps us develop greater patience, but it also might help us focus better and develop more self-control.[47] Would having patience, focus, and self-control be beneficial to our health? Without a doubt, they would, in addition to becoming better hunters. Play some chess now!

MUSIC

The sound of surrounding bugles is like beautiful music to elk hunters. A turkey hunter would love to hear a few nice gobbles here and there. What about the music we can create? Have you ever considered creating music of some kind? For many, making music has been avoided since third grade flute practice. For others, making music plays a special role in their lives by bringing together lovely harmonies that bring forth purely internal happiness.

The good news for us hunters is that making music, whether through singing or playing an instrument, may improve motor skills and working memory, which in turn boosts brain health.[48] As a result, it is reasonable to think of making music as a way to enhance our mental well-being.

Music has the power to influence our behavior. Have you ever experienced a state of bliss intertwined within your body and mind while listening to a certain song created by someone else? Where you have experienced sudden goosebumps and an overwhelming energy boost? I sure have. Your day can be entirely upgraded and changed by music, making you feel like you can conquer the world and succeed in whatever you do. It's a fantastic mood booster that we can utilize when we have a difficult day to assist us in getting through trouble or hardship.

The next time you're driving to your next hunt, turn on some music and get your singing on because you might be priming your brain to perform better on your hunt and elevate your health.

VISUAL ART

It's astonishing how long ago humans started depicting pictures of animals, battles, and hunts on the sides of rocks and caves. These art pieces have an abstract meaning that we still don't understand.

By articulating themselves through their art, people can make their thoughts and feelings known to others. Visual art can take on a variety of shapes and forms, whether it's inspired by your surroundings or purely conceptual. For instance, when I was a child, while at hunting camp, my mother would create beautiful baskets with deer horn sheds and other materials strung between them, while my father would create drawings of the current hunt on conks—fungal growths—found on nearby trees.

Art can be beautiful when there is flexibility and no restrictions on what a person can do. Flexibility fosters greater creativity, which is when we can achieve a state of total present-moment engagement. Creativity is possible for the spirit and purity of the heart to shine through when there are fewer patterns and rules we need to follow.

Jewelry, paintings, photography, writing, puzzles, and other forms of visual art have the potential to enhance thinking abilities, regulate heart rate, increase self-awareness, and even help handle stress levels.[49] Take an art class, remain at home, or go to the mountains for creative inspiration to express your thoughts and imagination and to help manage stress.

BACKUP HOBBIES

Something you are passionate about that is not your main hobby is referred to as a "backup hobby." Why is having a backup hobby important for hunters? Merely because your favorite hobby—hunting—could be taken away from you for various reasons, including ill health, physical injuries, changes in the laws, and so forth. What happens when you're unable to continue doing something you really enjoy, like pheasant hunting in South Dakota, for a variety of reasons? Realizing that you won't be able to continue engaging in that hobby that provides you so much joy can frequently cause a dark cloud to form in the mind, bringing with it feelings of anxiety and depression.

To ensure that our mental health stays robust, some level of stimulation and challenge for the mind is needed if life leads us in a different direction. This is why it is crucial to have a backup hobby or hobbies. Having a backup hobby can also help us become more well-rounded individuals and better athletes as hunters. Try participating in activities like fishing, bicycling, running, golf, and martial arts. All these activities can be quite applicable to hunting. The more physical activities we engage in, the more we can pick up on varied movement patterns, challenges, and experiences. All of these can help us develop better physical and mental skills for the hunt while also enhancing our health.

Let's explore surfing, one of my favorite backup hobbies. I've improved my health and hunting skills through surfing, and it also serves as an excellent backup hobby if I can't go hunting for whatever reason. When I was younger, my brothers, friends, and mentor Ray introduced me to surfing. Surfing originally comes from Hawaiian royalty and is sometimes referred to as the Sport of Kings. Our body, mind, and spirit can all be positively enhanced by ocean surfing in a variety of ways. What entices my attention and draws me to surfing are the mental and spiritual benefits. Numerous chemical reactions result from our immersion in the ocean while we surf. Our bodies can absorb the energy from water, as well as the minerals that start to rebalance our bodies' internal chemistry and general wellness. Surfing can aid in overcoming compulsive thinking by removing negative thoughts, overthinking, and emotional instability from the mind. The ocean is a great equalizer where spiritual health can be tapped into and cultivated. It's also good at providing us with new perspectives through surfing. We start to realize what's important and what is necessary for our life. If you've never had the chance to surf, know that tranquility and inner peace await you when you enter the ocean. No matter a person's age, race, gender, shape, or size, the ocean is a terrific place to rediscover oneself because it is completely neutral.

Now you can see how surfing is a backup hobby that could improve my hunting skills, enhance my health, and provide me something to do if hunting isn't an option for me for any reason. Any activity you choose, whether physically linked or not, can be a backup hobby. If movement is restricted for any reason, think about trying out new hobbies that call for fewer physical abilities, such as making music, painting, podcasting, reading, writing, and so forth.

A prime example of why we should have non-physically related hobbies in our lives is the mental health of many professional athletes who retire after playing physically demanding sports. When these athletes retire, many of them still have injuries from competing, which limits their range of motion and abilities. When this happens, the risk of depression can sometimes increase, especially if they lack other hobbies. To reduce the likelihood of mental health impairment, it is essential to have interests besides hunting that are both physically linked and unrelated to physical activity. We never know if we'll lose the ability to hunt.

LESS IS MORE

When we take a step back and reflect on our families, our jobs, and the things we do as a whole, we tend to notice unnecessary components added in. One of these, our possessions, might appear disorganized, cluttered, and overwhelming. This brings me to a crucial concept I acquired a few years ago, which has significantly enhanced the quality of my life. "Less is more." Less is more is encouraged by the concept of minimalism. Its foundation is supported by the idea that the more we value acquiring things, the less we appreciate what we currently have and ourselves. The belief that accumulating more things makes us happier and less stressed is where we must tread carefully. Why? Read on.

It's easy to become caught up in the habit of constantly purchasing new items to satisfy our boredom, to impress others, or because we believe that having that particular item would make us happier or less stressed. This is because our mind is greedy for more, which feeds the falsification of our self-worth when we obtain the item. That does not imply that we must always give in to this temptation and allow it to rule. If we continue to fuel the addiction of accumulating items to impress others or ourselves, we could fall into a dark vortex where nothing seems to make us happy or pleased. A mentality similar to status, accolades, and fame where we will never have enough. There is more to life than accumulating more material possessions.

Always chasing, buying, and accumulating more materialistic things won't fill the void of unhappiness and dissatisfaction in life. This makes sense given that once we obtain the desired item, we frequently lose interest in it after a few months, and our attention has now switched to another thing to buy, a.k.a. the hedonic treadmill. It's an illusion that turns us into slaves to our own stuff.

Consider this. If we buy a new bow every year, that does not guarantee that our archery-shooting abilities will improve. Investing in new workout equipment does not guarantee that we will improve our fitness. What could help is being consistent with shooting our bow and training. I know this is doable since I am becoming better at shooting with my "older" bow, and I train every day with a rusted barbell.

The situation is thus. Everywhere in the world, there is an abundance of workout equipment in garages. If you have one, carefully examine your workout space and ask yourself whether you are actually using the equipment. If you haven't used it in the last month, start doing so now, or sell or donate it. Now you can understand why getting new items won't make you successful or truly happy. If you put in the necessary effort and are consistent, you can achieve goals and be happy even with old or less equipment.

Even though they would be pleasant to have, new purchases of things are never the true solution to a potential issue and are merely momentary happiness enhancers. What I mean is this. If you're retired and have set aside money to buy a new rifle for hunting White-tailed deer in Texas, or if you have defective hunting gear like a broken archery sight and need a replacement, by all means, go ahead and make the purchase. Don't let me stop you from indulging in what you want. All I'll say is to ask yourself what your true motivation is for buying things. If the reason is that you are simply unhappy or stressed out in life, you might want to reconsider, as you are only treating the symptoms and not the root of the problem.

The feeling of discontent that results from desiring more things is frequently caused by a problem with mental health rather than a desire for the things themselves. Real and long-term happiness, a sense of security, and strong mental health are not achieved through a never-ending pursuit of more materialistic possessions. Living with less, showing genuine gratitude for what we have, fostering relationships with others, pushing yourself, engaging in experiences, helping others, and learning from life's mistakes all contribute to well-being and better mental health.

We must understand that the quality of our lives is not determined by the number of possessions we own, the amount of money we earn, the quality of our vehicle, the size of our home, the style of our wardrobe, etc. If it were, a lot more people would be happy and with good mental health. Our state of physical, mental, and spiritual health (*Your Hunting Healthspan*) determines the quality of our life. The quality of life we are actually living is shown by the energy, joy, and ease we feel on the inside.

Being aware of our purchases and having good justifications for them is the first step in adopting the less-is-more concept. Do we need X, or is it just a minor want? There is a difference between a want and a need. It's up to you to decide what that is. Next, take a good, honest look around your home and consider whether you utilize each item you have and what its purpose is. Look through your closet for clothing and be honest with yourself about how frequently you wear what you have. In the most recent month or months, have you actually worn X? If not, you might want to get rid of it. Your office, garage, vehicle, pantry, refrigerator, attic, and other spaces in your home may also be worth organizing and decluttering.

Then, set aside an entire month once a year to sell the items you hardly ever use or need or, even better, donate them to someone who could use them more than you do. I've given away a lot of clothes I didn't need to local kids who were overjoyed to be able to wear more than one T-shirt in a week. Donating reduces the clutter in our life while also allowing us to feel more liberated and happy by helping others.

Maybe make it a rule for yourself to get rid of something from your home whenever you buy something. In that sense, it's an exchange. In this manner, there can be a balance between your possessions and the number of items in your home.

Consider the items that are consistently handed down from one generation to the next. There might be a few meaningful things, but the vast bulk of the things we own are probably not going to be useful to others once we pass away. The few things I've retained from family and friends who have passed away are very special to me, quality over quantity.

One of the main reasons it may be difficult for us to eliminate items and adopt a minimalist outlook is the simple belief that going through our possessions would be a waste of time. It is crucial to understand that when we are not decluttering and organizing our belongings, we may experience increased stress and anxiety due to the numerous, overwhelming items we possess. Bringing less-is-more into our life doesn't require specific training, money, or particular skills, just consistent effort and self-discipline. Instead of continually wanting more things, let's be grateful for what we already have and the people in our life—live simply.

TIME

According to life and how we age, minutes are precious currencies on this planet. Having less time implies there might be fewer opportunities to go hunting. Because of this, we can't hope for a change in our physical, mental, or spiritual well-being. If we want our health to improve, we must actively utilize time by continuously learning, putting it to use, and coming up with ways to make the most of it. One of the time-related topics that needs to be explored in regard to our health is what we do during the workweek. This is why.

To get to the weekend, many want Monday through Friday to pass quickly. Once the weekend arrives, it rushes by them. The dwelling of the workweek of doing something they don't enjoy sometimes follows. This cycle is on repeat until they reach retirement, where most of their life has been lived already.

Hoping for Monday through Friday to go by fast during a typical week is another way of wishing our life to go by faster. One reason we may want our workweek to end quickly is that our boss or coworkers are making us feel stressed. If so, think about applying some of the tactics from Chapter 1 to manage chronic stress better. If we want every day to feel like the weekend, we could also work on changing what we are doing Monday through Friday. It is worth the effort and time if doing that means working on a side project or looking for new job opportunities before or after work, especially to improve our mental well-being and happiness. We can't get time back, and it's not guaranteed in terms of how long we will live.

If changing what you do from Monday through Friday is not an option for any reason, at the very least, take care of your health. By doing this, we can at least be able to enjoy retirement while having plenty of energy, happiness, and opportunities for hunting, like in California for waterfowl. A lot of people begin to retire around age sixty-five. In the US, the average life expectancy is around eighty, so we may live another fifteen years. Which is still not guaranteed by the time we retire simply because we have not been taking care of ourselves via healthy lifestyle choices.

> Poor health defeats the purpose of retirement.

Fifteen years that are not even guaranteed due to the quality of our health that we spent thirty years working toward does not sound ideal for experiencing what life can be. Unfortunately, I am aware of individuals who were affected by this and who later passed away from a chronic disease right after they retired. Take care of your health to set yourself up for present and future success.

If you've already retired, try to lead a healthier lifestyle to live a greater quality of life. Find a new goal, sleep well, challenge yourself, be active, feed your mind with good reading, consume nourishing foods, spend time with your family, and do what you love. We only get one chance at this life game, so make the most of it by taking advantage of your well-earned retirement by exploring everything life has to offer. Every day offers a chance to reprogram our minds to improve our circumstances with less regret. Ask a centenarian; your life will go faster than you could have ever imagined.

Transferring bear meat across a river using a pulley system.

In relation to the future and time, my memories are one of the things I cherish the most as I get older. This image holds a memory that will always be treasured. As you'll see, the photo is a little bit hazy because I was taking it when my brother and I were engaged in an activity on the opposite side of the river. To put it shortly, I harvested a black bear at the base of a cliff across a river. There were a couple of ways my brother and I could get the bear.

The first option involved returning to camp on foot and traversing several mountains to reach the other side. Our calculations indicated that it would take, at best, three to four hours to descend the cliffs and difficult terrain. Putting our crocs on and wading across the river was option two, which wasn't really an option. With the depth and ferocity of the river in our line of sight, I quickly rejected this option. Our attention was about to go to option one when my brother suggested option three. The third option wouldn't take long, and if I did it perfectly, no one would get wet. Easier said than done, right?

I thus chose the third option, which was to shimmy across a log that had fallen across the river. Naturally, it wasn't a tree with no branches. It was home to many limbs that protruded in varying directions. I have a history with logs, so let's just say my brother had to persuade me a little. As a result, I shimmied over a log directly above the swiftly flowing river to start my quest to find the bear meat that I so desperately wanted. I reached the other side in approximately ten minutes. I started side-hilling till I reached the bear after getting to the other side.

My brother had the brilliant idea to construct a pulley system using a 550 cord directly across the river, as can be seen in the photo. We fastened the cord to a nearby tree, then transferred the bear meat and all of my equipment in a waterproof container back and forth until all of it was on the other side. It was one of those moments where we were so excited we started laughing with happiness. After we were done, I crossed the river again on the log, and the rest is history.

This image also makes me think of the unpredictable weather we often had when out bear hunting in the spring. We experienced rain, sunshine, warmth, fog, snow, hail, and blue sky in less than an hour on this trip. If you hunt in regions where the weather is, at best, unpredictable, you need to protect your equipment from the elements so that your rifle, for example, can still function. For a scope and crown cover that is lightweight and durable for all weather conditions, check out the StHealthy Hunter rifle cover.

CHALLENGE YOURSELF

Regret ranks among the saddest internal feelings one can have. The famous line, "I wish I would have..." can be quite common to hear as we age. Regret can drastically alter how we view life, as well as the potential to experience joy and happiness. If you don't believe me, go to a nearby senior center and talk to the residents.

The tendency to take the easy path and avoid taking on new challenges in life is one of the major causes of regret. The likely reasons include getting too comfortable, fear of failing, playing it safe, and worrying about what other people might say.

When we give thought to it, what other people think of us regarding the challenges we take on doesn't really matter in the grand scheme of life. Having the fear of failure when we try anything new could lead to us living a less meaningful life than what we truly desire. By staying within our comfort zone, we risk stagnating and missing out on opportunities to develop individually and experience more of life.

For instance, I could have easily decided not to write this book because I knew it would be extremely difficult for me to complete. Once it began to take longer than I had anticipated, I could have easily given up. My ninety-year-old self would have said something to the effect of, "I should have gone for it" or "I should have never quit no matter how long it was going to take" if I had taken the easier path in either situation. I know this in my heart. Both of those responses result from regret, which I want to experience less of in my lifetime.

Have I ever had a thought—or thoughts—like those examples? Without a doubt. When things get challenging, that is sometimes the reality. The point is, though, I constantly told myself how proud I would be of my efforts in the future, no matter the outcome. The choice of what I wanted and needed to do then seemed quite clear. To avoid regret later in life, pursue challenging tasks. When we push ourselves, those moments are usually some of the best life experiences. If you need suggestions for ways to challenge yourself, consider the following:

Ideas for Ways to Challenge Yourself	
Train every day.	Develop a solution to keep wild game cool in hot conditions.
Develop a solution for preventing tick bites.	
Sign up for a marathon.	Hunt a different location every year.
Develop a solution to reduce chronic-wasting disease.	
	Take a cold shower every day.
Develop a solution for keeping public land trash-free.	Develop a solution to reduce human trafficking.
Shoot your bow/rifle every week.	Wait till 3:00 p.m. to look at mainstream social media.
Develop a solution to reduce poaching.	
Read a chapter a day of a book.	Develop a solution for keeping our oceans trash-free.
Develop a solution to reduce domestic abuse.	
Develop a solution to reduce hoof rot disease.	Start a business that positively contributes to the hunting community.
Follow a specific dietary regimen for an entire year.	
	Complete a twenty-minute stillness session every day.
Develop a solution for wheelchairs to be more accessible.	No TV on the weekends for an entire year.
Static stretch for at least ten minutes every day.	

How difficult of a challenge you choose to take on is entirely up to you. I listed a range of challenges because of this. Whatever you want to do, regardless of what happens, can help you grow and lessen regret. It's okay to fail when trying new things. I've failed ten times as much as I've succeeded. Never give up, and keep going forward. Fail 100 times, rise up 101 times.

Remember that waiting for things to improve might never happen because life is meant to be lived. No matter what happens, taking action is always better than waiting. No matter how often we fail, trying harder and taking on new challenges is a good idea. Remember that we only get one life to live.

BE AUTHENTIC

When we worry about what other people think of us, strive to be someone we are not, or allow the people we surround ourselves with to change the essence of who we are, we are further drawn away from the health and life we desire and the hunting opportunities we long for. Focusing on oneself and being authentic with our personality and ideals through true self-expression could be considered a superpower because it is so rare these days.

There is a good chance that at some point in our life, someone or some individuals may attempt to degrade us or transform us into something they desire. This frequently occurs because people of this type are probably internally broken and are attempting to transfer some of that negative energy onto someone else. In actuality, if we are truly comfortable with who we are, we shouldn't give a damn about what other people think. That person down the street who said that negative opinion to you about how you shoot your bow is not you; that's them.

Imagine yourself at eighty-seven years of age. Do you think you will be able to name every person whose opinions you were concerned about in the prior thirty years? Most likely, you will not. This teaches us that it doesn't matter what people think of us for doing or saying. Just be authentic and live your life as you like.

There could be many causes for why we care so much about what people think of us. Whatever the reason, I'm going to share with you something to think about. If no one has told you already, these people who we are worried about what they think of us are actually not even thinking about us, to begin with. They are actually concerned with their own problems and are also worried about what you think about them. It's a full circle where everyone worries about what others think about them. Quite the mind-bender, right? Contrary to what we may believe, no one is actually thinking about us on a regular basis. Break the cycle by focusing on yourself instead; it could radically change the way you view and experience life.

Finally, prioritize your own needs by surrounding yourself with growth-minded people who are enhancing their physical, mental, and spiritual well-being. The individuals who encourage you to be your authentic self and to be driven, humble, healthy, optimistic, honest, and kind. Let's go over several matters related to authenticity that you ought to be aware of.

Society

It is vital to realize that society can be quite good at driving us into predetermined patterns and behavior routes so that we conform to its expectations. All of this reflects how society is attempting to fit us into the "most acceptable" piece of the puzzle. If we are not fully conscious of what is going on, it is easy to become dragged in without noticing it.

There are various ways that society can push us to conform to, be persuaded by, feel peer pressure, push us to focus on self-image, and decide if we are socially acceptable based on specific norms, depending on where we are located and what is thought to be "normal."

Not everything society has come to accept as normal is bad. If we look for it, there is also good there. In any case, I want you to realize that a person has the most power when they are free to be who they are and to express themselves in any way they see fit. Once we realize this, we can feel much more empowered to act and live how we want instead of how society expects us to.

When you are authentic, you get to choose what to "normalize." You are in charge because you don't care what other people think of you. Be free, wear whatever you please, style your hair as you want, etc. Seeing someone express themselves honestly and openly the way they want to always brings a smile to my face because it is not always easy to do.

Friends

As we age, we tend to associate with people who share common interests and sometimes even exhibit similar traits to ourselves. One of my favorite things about the hunting community is that. Connecting and collaborating with other hunters who are passionate about this way of life is invigorating. Even though you are probably already aware, there are still things to be cautious of in relation to our friends, particularly during the off-season, which may have an impact on our authenticity and even well-being.

We can start by examining the kind of friends we surround ourselves with. Think about the discussions you have and the topics that are brought up. Regardless of what's said, it's crucial to know we can unconsciously adopt any of these language patterns and character traits and begin using them to express ourselves without even noticing it. To some extent, the quality of your conversations with friends might shape you into someone who resembles how your friends act and talk.

Perhaps we've had a challenging day at work and need to vent, so be it. The important thing to realize in interactions with our friends is how frequently we express certain thoughts. Maybe reassess things when a talk that started out negative turns into a habit.

Not that we need to cut ties with certain friends, but it's good to be aware of the minor things that could get in the way of our ability to be authentic. Some examples of conversations between friends that can negatively affect our authenticity include gossip, making fun of others, complaining about others, blaming others for one's problems, finding the bad in things, and talking badly behind others' backs. This is especially true if it occurs frequently.

Picture yourself with a group of friends who use one of the conversational traits I listed. In my opinion, we have a great opportunity to influence this situation by stepping up and changing the conversation's direction. With something like a positive and productive conversation where we talk about our goals and ideas, recall happy moments, or ask for guidance in specific areas of our life, we can take the initiative to change the direction of the conversation. If we regularly act, we might even be able to create a real, long-lasting shift. The other option is to avoid those who consistently exhibit these poor conversational traits. By using this strategy and looking in the mirror, we might discover that some of our friends have drifted away precisely because of these conversational tendencies.

All these conversational traits not only make being authentic more challenging, but they can also alter who we are at our core, negatively impact our mental health, and disrupt our course in life. Be authentic, express better traits, and set an example for your friends. Remember that what counts is progress, not perfection.

Online Influencers

Thanks to the internet and social media apps, we now have access to many influencers. Some of these folks, but not all of them, are portraying wonderful attributes. In any case, there are a few things to look out for from these people that can divert you from being authentic. One thing to watch out for is the inclination to adopt these influencers' traits to the degree that we begin to alter who we are as individuals and behave in their manner.

If this occurs, our authenticity may begin to fade, which can drive us to become consumed with our appearance to the point where we lose sight of who we truly are, resulting in a false identity and later unhappiness. The important thing is to avoid trying to live our lives exactly like someone we see online. It's possible to continuously be yourself and gain inspiration from exemplary role models simultaneously.

The concept of comparison is another aspect to be mindful of because it endangers our authenticity. No matter how well things are going for us, comparing our life to others we see online could cause envy, steal our joy and happiness, destroy our confidence, make us feel less grateful, and even somewhat impede how we are experiencing life. When we least suspect it, comparing ourselves to others can catch us off guard and change our attitude, emotions, and behavior toward others. It can lead to us complaining and making fun of others to make ourselves feel better. The drawback is that if this happens, we dig ourselves further into an illusion.

Analyze your life and search for moments where the sneaky comparison is creeping up on you. If it happens, pull away while announcing "no more." Your ancestors will smile if you put the phone aside and take time to reflect and rebalance inside.

Online Critics (a.k.a. Tiny Little Flies)

This hunting lifestyle comes with individuals criticizing us for what we do because of their beliefs. Just because someone criticizes us online doesn't mean we have to let them take our energy. It might be easy to respond to these critics with a typed message to break their spirit, but that doesn't mean that's the only course of action. When we reply to online critics by trying to belittle or make fun of them, we take a step closer to becoming someone who loses sight of who they really are (less authentic), which is exactly what the critic wants.

No matter if they are writing negative remarks on our online profile about the type of camo we wear, how we bugle, how we train, the kind of pack we have, the size of wild game we have harvested, etc. Critics want us to invest our energy and time in a retaliating response to their comment—it's a trick. When we respond to them out of unpleasant emotions, our ability to reason and use logic is hampered.

If you must respond, be neutral, optimistic, and uplifting. Offer them a new perspective, educate them, or wish them the best. Maybe the criticism happens to be constructive feedback that can improve your position. Reach out and thank them for it if this is the case. Perhaps the comment indicated a threat to you or your family (quite common actually). Make the best decision you can under the circumstances, depending on the situation's specifics and its seriousness. In general, try your best to keep your composure when you hear comments from individuals trying to divert you off the path you are on.

> There are times during a horse's lifetime when tiny, annoying flies land on them. Keep an eye on them because sometimes they swat them away, and other times they simply show no reaction and carry on with their actions. In either case, they typically don't lose control and let them alter their energies. Regarding critics' opinions that seem negative, act like a horse.

Here's how to evaluate whether this tactic is effective. Think about the seventeen most recent times you encountered negative comments online. Do you remember the specifics of what happened, including the person, setting, words, emotions, and date, in chronological order? Most likely not. In fact, in a few short years, the entire incident will be forgotten. It is, therefore, unimportant in the grand scheme of things. These are not significant events in our lives, even though we mistakenly think they are. I find it hard to comprehend that when we are ninety-one years of age, we will still be thinking about these critics and what they said to us.

Instead of "calling out" and criticizing others, or trying to prove people wrong who disagree with our ideals, way of life, the fact that we hunt, and other things, let's put our energy into something else. Let's focus on ourselves and how we can put our energies into different ways to improve our lives. In light of how fast time flies, I think this is a helpful strategy for our mental health, general well-being, authenticity, and serves as an excellent example for the next generation of hunters.

Mentors

Depending on how you were raised in this world, you may or may not have had people who could help and guide you through difficult times and help you learn things as you grew older. Some people seek advice and direction from family members or close family friends. I somehow managed to fall into this group after my father passed away with family friends Jay and Ray, who served as my mentors when I was young and are still doing so now. The question is: what should a person do if they cannot find a mentor or advisor?

Fortunately, there are plenty of free videos and podcasts with "possible mentors" available on the internet. The availability of mentoring through these online tools gives us the chance to learn from others even if we never get the chance to meet or interact with them in person. We can search for and find the people who best fit our unique needs and what we are seeking, thanks to this access.

It's important to remember that we don't have to agree with everything a person says. You get to choose what you want to adhere to (much like this mere book). You have the power to gather various informational tidbits that you deem to be valuable and store them as you see fit while staying authentic. In some ways, it's like shopping for the mentoring and guidance you want.

When actively seeking a mentor online, search for those who are inspiring, humble, optimistic, healthy, eager to help others, kind, and authentic. It's worthwhile to spend the time to listen to these folks and learn something from them that can improve our health and quality of life, drive us, or open our eyes to a different perspective.

WHOLENESS > HAPPINESS

A key component in the equation for achieving optimal health is experiencing happiness. Understanding the discourse that Gautama Buddha, a teacher in India around the fifth century BCE, had with a person is one method to live a happier life. A man stated to Gautama Buddha, "I want happiness." The Buddha advised, "First remove 'I,' that's ego, then remove 'want,' that's desire. See now you are left with only 'happiness.'" We can rewire our brains to immerse ourselves in genuine happiness if we can comprehend the principles of that discussion on a basic level and apply them to our lives.

Happiness is a wonderful feeling. We can experience it to varying degrees by being around particular friends and loved ones, hitting our aim perfectly, achieving our goals, going on our annual hunts, and other situations that feel fulfilling, among other things. There are a number of components in this book that can make us happier on various levels. The issue is that I frequently see how others' feelings of happiness are affected when someone else performs worse than they do. Then, egotistical self-esteem increases. I find this to be a sad and unhealthy way to live.

When we feel happy about someone else doing poorly to make ourselves feel better, this sounds to me like a road that may result in a buildup of negative internal energy, anxiety, and depression in addition to a false sense of short-term satisfaction. If someone adopted this as their default behavior, I would wager to guess that they might experience an imbalance and oppressive feeling of thoughts and emotions. Doesn't it make sense to concentrate on doing everything we can to improve our ability to experience happiness while also wishing others happiness?

The question is what happens when life becomes gloomy, dismal, and less good? There will be many times in life when it can be challenging to stay happy. At this point, wholeness shows up. Accepting all that happens to us is a core part of wholeness, including our achievements (happiness), our failures (shortcomings), and everything in between. While happiness is good, wholeness becomes superior once we embrace it, as it teaches us.

Life's problems can bring us down into a state of discontentment, sorrow, and low self-worth if we let them. There will be times when you feel like giving up, that everything is going wrong, and that the world is crumbling around you. Believe me, I've been there. Some of you have likely gone through experiences in life that are beyond comprehension. Worse than anything I've ever encountered.

There is no doubt that everyone will experience challenging or unexpected circumstances at some point in their life. The only distinction is that depending on the person and the situation, different levels of sadness, disappointment, and so forth occur. Maybe we get hit with an unexpected bill, a family member passes away, or we get hurt just before our once-in-a-lifetime hunt for Bighorn sheep. Although these low points are unpleasant, they can also provide us the chance to learn more about life and ourselves, to appreciate things more, and to learn things that can help us grow as better-quality individuals.

Even though things may appear to be only negative, if we really look for them, life may have something to teach us. Everything that happens to us—the good times, the bad times, and everything in between—is there so we can fully experience life. This is precisely how we can start fostering wholeness—by adopting a new outlook on accepting life's highs, lows, and unpleasant moments that we will all experience to some degree. To create harmony and balance in our lives, we must embrace wholeness.

Ways #52–64 to Age Better and Prevent Disease

52. Always and forever be a student for life and aim for more clarity.
53. Read more books.
54. Get your chess game on.
55. Explore methods of making music.

56. Cultivate visual art to express yourself and your thoughts.

57. Partake in a backup hobby or hobbies.

58. Adopt and incorporate less is more (minimalism) into all areas of life.

59. Reestablish a new relationship with time.

60. Avoid putting yourself in positions of regret; apply consistent effort into all things.

61. Seek challenging tasks regularly to experience more of life.

62. Be more authentic and focus on yourself, not others' opinions.

63. Find mentors who can give you advice, support, and guidance.

64. Embrace wholeness.

CHAPTER 7

TAKE A LOOK OUTSIDE THE BINOCULARS

Enjoy the Journey and Continually Improve

By looking in your binoculars, you can see a mule deer's hair composition from the opposite side of the mountain. When you pull your binoculars away from your face, you see the land surrounding the deer, the clouds, the birds, the geometrical space between you, the mountain, and the universe. Step back far enough, and you might have a better point of view of our significance and the bigger picture of hunting and life. The bigger picture is the *process*.

One of the best parts of this self-improvement journey is the process that brings the results to better health and experiencing more hunting opportunities. It's the time between starting to make better lifestyle choices and achieving the goals you have made for yourself. It's everything that occurs from start to finish, whether it be good, bad, or ugly. Our experiences, choices we must make, ups and downs, unforeseen happenings, and so forth. They are all a part of the process.

To attain our results and goals, it is imperative that we accept this notion of the process. Believe it or not, the body, mind, and spirit all desire to be in good health. All we need to do is be consistent and practice patience while working toward our goals, and everything will work out as it should.

On this health and life journey sometimes things go our way and other times they don't. Understand, though, it's all a part of the process, including adversity. Adversity is not all bad; it can be a steppingstone to learning more about self, and that is beneficial. Straining a muscle or having functionality issues with our compound bow on our hunting trip is only temporary and does not mean it's the end of the world. It means we now have an opportunity to learn the importance of stretching to prevent muscular strains and to bring back up parts for our compound bow to camp.

I have failed, lost, and been tested by adversity way more in health, hunting, and life than I have succeeded. From tearing my meniscus, and missing a shot at a monster black bear with my bow, to experiencing the death of my father and most of my family members, and so on. But because I was looking for lessons to learn in any situation, they all helped me grow as a person.

Undoubtedly, many people have dealt with adversity in situations that were considerably more challenging than mine. In light of this, it's good to be aware that there is always adversity in life, despite what it may seem when we see someone achieve something, whether it be improving their health or harvesting mature wild game. Usually, there is more to a story than what you initially see or hear. While each person's process is extremely different, we can all adhere to a similar principle for seeing adversity as a learning opportunity.

You see, life will be filled with adversity, difficulty, and defeat. However, it is up to us to embrace these moments or let them dictate our long-term reality. Life rarely goes according to our plans, so how we respond is important.

Consider this story of overcoming adversity:

My father once left early in the morning for a day hunt up in logging country during the archery elk season with the intention of returning in the late afternoon in time to teach four classes at his martial arts school. He decides to get one last hike in before having to return to town in the late afternoon. While on this stroll through a patch of thick ferns, he ended up falling down a short slope. Somehow, while he was falling, a wood arrow popped out from his longbow quiver, and the broadhead of the arrow passed through his calf muscle (gastrocnemius) and out the other side. Picture a skewer. To stop the bleeding, he decided to break each side of the arrow such that a few inches still remained in the calf. He followed that by covering it with some gauze and duct tape. He arrived back just in time to teach his classes which implied that he had never visited the hospital beforehand. In fact, he didn't tell his black belt students or show any signs of pain, so they were unaware of what he had been through. My father didn't admit what had happened until after his final class when one of the black belts, who would later become one of his closest friends, observed blood dripping from my father's shoe. My father intended to set an example of conquering adversity by using the "will," thus he did not want to cancel any of the classes or inform any of his students. He wanted to apply what he preached to his students. In truth, he did exactly that. There is a lesson to be learned here, though. Later, when his students heard what had transpired, they realized how powerful the "will" could be in the face of adversity. They discovered and truly learned the "will" had power, as my father demonstrated. Adversity may be a great teacher, in fact. And yes, that evening, after finishing all of his classes, my father went to the hospital to receive stitches and have the remaining arrow removed. I do not suggest that you react to a circumstance like this in the same way that my father did. This is just a story.

> Once we understand and recognize that obstacles, failures, mistakes, and losses are all disguised as learning opportunities, it is then that we can begin to realize these unfortunate moments can be a step toward something better, if we want them to be.

Recognize the value of every moment of the process, no matter how beautiful or terrible it is. Our success and capacity to change perspectives on health and life, in general, can be considerably improved after we internalize this framework. Embrace the process; everything that occurs is a part of getting to our results and goals.

PERSPECTIVES

It appears that when problems and difficulties arise, our outlook can become narrowed. This is a typical human reaction that many people have experienced, including me. The problem is that when our outlook narrows frequently and uncontrollably, it increases the likelihood that we will say or do something out of reactive emotions rather than being strategic or methodical. Not that we must always react perfectly to life's challenges. Nevertheless, there are ways to alter our outlook on situations that are not turning out as we had hoped, regardless of our current position.

Shifting our perspective can be one approach to assist us in dealing with a tough situation and seeing it from a different point of view. From a different perspective, we might realize that other individuals have likely faced and overcome situations that are both similar to and worse than our own. This type of thinking is crucial for how we experience life since it tells us that anything is possible. Undoubtedly a critical strength that can significantly improve our health and quality of life is the ability to change our perspective.

Influential aspects of our lives, such as our habits, families, the difficulties we face, the people we associate with, the things we read and listen to, the challenges we take on, our adventures, and our exposure to nature, can help us cultivate different perspectives. We simply need to make sure we make the most of the countless resources of knowledge, environments, and people that are available to us to keep our perspectives from being too limited.

Thinking about our significance in this world can help us develop fresh perspectives as well. The minor things in life, such as the money we had to spend, the email we forgot to send, or the hunting mishaps that didn't go as planned, may not mean as much as we first believed if we realize that we live on a planet floating in the universe that we don't know much about. Less significant than we think is the blown stock on that big Rocky Mountain bull elk in Montana. Yes, it's unfortunate that this occurred. However, since it is so insignificant in this thing called life, there is no need to dwell on it.

Or, conceptualize this if you want to take it a step further. There is a very slim chance that at the age of ninety-two, you will recall the incident in which your neighbor backed into your brand-new car forty years ago. There is a much higher likelihood that at ninety-two, you will reflect on the time you spent with loved ones, the lessons you learned, the experiences you had, how you helped others, and how you lived. This reveals to us what matters and what doesn't in the brief time we have here on earth.

When we acknowledge that we are not the most important life form on this planet, we can also get a broader perspective on life. Given the crucial role bees play in maintaining a balanced ecosystem, it wouldn't be long until all other living things, including humans, cease to exist if all bees in the world perish tomorrow. All other living things, however, would continue to flourish and prosper if all humans on the planet perished tomorrow. Since we play a much smaller role in creation than we realize, our daily hassles and frustrations are far less important.

Me with a black-tailed deer backstrap.

Last fall, I was fortunate to go rifle hunting for black-tailed deer with a good buddy where I grew up. Like most hunting trips, there is always something to learn. During this trip, I learned I should practice different shooting positions with my rifle, just like my bow. Earlier in the morning, I had missed a blacktail while attempting an offhand shot. A shooting position I have never practiced. Luckily during this trip, I got another chance, and this time, I made sure I put myself in a shooting position where I felt more comfortable (prone), which allowed me to connect on a nice blacktail.

I am starting to think that practicing different shooting positions with our rifles is imperative to performing a successful shot, especially when we recognize all of the potential terrain variables and situations that can occur while on the hunt. Not only is it important to improve our accuracy in various shooting positions, but also I have found it beneficial to replicate a real hunting scenario by elevating our heart rate before we take a shot. One of the facets of shooting that has helped me prepare for hunts better is using some form of training (i.e., running, burpees, rower, etc.) that elevates the heart rate right before I shoot during target practice so I can replicate a closer, more realistic hunting situation.

This was also when I began appreciating a well-designed bipod for my rifle created by Spartan Precision. Not only was my rifle extremely stable while I rested it on a stump, but this ultralight bipod also allowed me to pivot on a swivel, so if the deer had moved to the left or right, I could have still moved with it while still being locked into the bipod. The way gear advances every year is unbelievable at times.

PURPOSE

Since the beginning of civilization, many have been actively trying to find or determine their purpose in life. The thing they are meant to be doing (a.k.a. the riddle of life). Personally, I'm not sure having a specific purpose is required to live a good quality of life full of vitality. Without being aware of their purpose, many people I've known lead very fulfilling lives by simply being present in the moment. However, if one is interested in this subject and begins to invest effort in discovering their own personal purpose, they may start to develop a strong internal feeling that might inspire them to live life well beyond what they had previously imagined feasible.

I was first exposed to this idea of *What is your purpose?* while going through college. Those days, I came up with many different answers that I conveyed to my professors and classmates. It's a great conversation piece to get the mind thinking in a particular way, especially at a younger age. But it's also incredibly difficult to talk about and answer honestly. Should a younger individual be able to construct an answer effectively? Possibly or not. Do your family or friends know your purpose? Possibly or not. I'm not sure if there is a particular age by which we should have an answer. When we think about it, we might never have an answer, or we might have an answer right away.

Even though this is a difficult question to answer, I believe that the answer is out there; it may just take some time and sincere thought to discover it. Perhaps instead of asking ourselves what we should be doing, maybe we need to ask ourselves what is most important to us personally. I believe two approaches are both extremely good for figuring out our unique purposes. Let's discuss the first approach: using our passion for inspiring and helping others.

Whatever our passion, if we have a strong, deep connection to it, we can use it as our purpose. How? When we have a deep connection to something that makes us happy, it allows us to share it with others who share our interests. Sharing our knowledge, excitement, and experiences with others can encourage them to join us in our endeavors and may even improve their lives somehow. Helping and inspiring others through our passion and living life in terms of what we can add to the world (hence, this book) can bring a feeling of joy that feels unreal and ecstatic (a.k.a. fulfilled). I certainly feel that way when I assist others in improving their physical, mental, and spiritual health.

Perhaps you haven't yet identified your passion. That's okay. Start thinking carefully about the things you love doing more of. Start looking into various lifestyles, subjects, and topics online to see if anything stirs your interest. If the internet's massive amount of search results appears too overwhelming, there is an alternative. Since it is so underrated, it is actually my favorite. The name of it is the public library. You can explore from a practical standpoint by going to your local public library. My hunch is that somewhere on those shelves is the passion you aspire to get involved with. Start looking around; you never know what you may find.

The second approach to serve as our purpose is something that all of us can use and set as our guide. And that is the journey of life itself. Using the journey of life itself as our purpose is when we recognize all of the magnificent and incredible things in life that we can become aware of. It involves paying more attention to and immersing oneself in the countless things that exist in life, such as the amazing qualities of nature, traveling to new locations, various experiences, reviewing history, information found in books, the marvelous things we can create, etc. It is then that we can be engaged with an everlasting willingness to learn and expand ourselves, thus, a purpose.

When the journey of life itself is our purpose, we will explore as many aspects of this life as we can, especially our internal self. You will find this approach is non-limiting. Every day we can wake up with aliveness and energy. We can look at each day as a possibility to discover more of what life has to offer. If we take this path, we won't feel stuck in life as often.

Regardless of the path you choose for your purpose, both using your passion for inspiring and helping others and using the journey of life itself may provide your life with a strong sense of meaning, fulfillment, and robust mental health.

POTENTIAL

Often, when we think we know what our potential is, it's constructed in a way that there is an end goal. Like having the thought that once we harvest an eight-point Whitetail in Georgia, we have reached our potential. But what happens once we reach our perceived potential? Then what?

Often, we evaluate others around us or someone we look up to as the framework for figuring out what this so-called potential for ourselves might be. I'm not sure if this is the best approach. I'm also not sure if we really even know what our potential is at times. More often than not, I think we underestimate our capabilities, I believe, because of the experiences we have had and the people and things we have been exposed to throughout our lives.

After much reflection, it seems to me that our potential has no ceiling.

> In other words, the sky is not the limit. The limit is ourselves.

As long as we keep trying to get better, there is no end to our potential. The reality is that as soon as we reach the point where we initially believed our potential lay, it changes. Because of this, the notion that "we made it" has no value. "Here we are, where to now?" is more appropriate.

Once we accomplish what we thought we were capable of in terms of our goals, our potential then becomes reestablished over and over again. It never ends or concludes; it is only temporary if we want it to be. Keyword: if. With this in mind, think about what you have gleaned as your potential. Do you think it's something unattainable? Do you think you underestimate yourself? Nobody knows the answer for you. But if you're wondering, all you have to do is be willing to keep pushing your capabilities toward this supposed potential by accomplishing goals to determine how much worth it actually carries. I'm going to venture a guess that you are more than capable of going beyond what you originally believed. That is, if you persist in cultivating an obsession with pushing yourself to limits you never imagined possible via sacrifice, perseverance, and hard work.

Remember, we only get one life. No more waiting around hoping that your current position gets better for you. Get on a better path right now. Reduce as many unnecessary distractions as you can that take up your energy. Every day, take at least one step in the right direction. Keep going no matter how many steps it takes. Put that effort on repeat. Crush your goals. This is how we take our physical, mental, and spiritual health to newer heights. This is how we can get closer to what we think our potential is.

GRATITUDE

Until something goes wrong, we may not fully appreciate the things we have, such as access to food, clean water, air, shelter, the capacity to communicate, move around, see, have relationships, and the ability to pursue wild game. All these things are blessings; therefore, we should appreciate them and never take them for granted. Genuine joy, happiness, and a better quality of life result from practicing gratitude in daily life. Let's dive deeper.

Traveling and exposing oneself to new environments and circumstances is one of the best ways to enhance our sense of gratitude for the things in our life. When I was younger, I had the great privilege of being invited by a high school sports coach on a mission trip to Ensenada, Mexico, to assist with the building of a small house for a family of nine. When we got there, this family, a mother, and eight kids lived in a cardboard and tarp structure. My eyes saw hardship and struggle as they managed without many of the comforts that some people wouldn't think twice about. In terms of experiences, I am sure many of you have seen things far more intense than I have. These experiences can mold us into more grateful people once we become vulnerable to them and have a genuine reflection on them.

Growing up, I didn't have it anywhere near as tough as that family in Mexico did. But after some reflection, I realize that I am much more grateful for life's little comforts. When I was younger, my family and I resided in a log home where power outages were common due to storms. We had no heating other than our wood fireplace. Inside our home, my breath was visible, making the coldness obvious. We frequently used candles and propane lanterns to generate enough light to maintain vision. I seem to remember that elk fur skins were frequently used as blankets. The floors frequently became damp because of the roof's continual leaks. When my parents asked me to go outside and get firewood, it typically involved getting drenched in rain, stepping in peacock and dog poop from our Great Pyrenees, watching out for that black cougar that frequently crossed our property, and being extra cautious for the black widows that frequently made their homes in the wood stack. Because my father was once bitten, I always feared grabbing wood. At the time, all these things appeared to be life-limiting. My childhood discomfort still pales compared to what that family in Mexico went through. After giving it some serious thought, I've come to the realization that all of these childhood experiences contributed to my current state of gratitude, where I value even the smallest things in life more. My level of gratitude in life is significantly higher because of my upbringing.

Sometimes all it takes to cultivate gratitude is exposure to one special individual. A person I met a few years back has significantly changed my life. Owen is his name. Owen is one of the most, if not the toughest, sincere people I have ever met. Due to his rare genetic condition, Owen has challenges with daily activities like verbally communicating and moving independently.

Owen is one of the first people I think of when I'm going through a difficult time. Even while some of life's difficulties may seem severe or tough to overcome, they are nothing compared to what Owen goes through every day of his life. Even though he faces difficulties, he smiles, never gives up, and inspires many others, including myself. Owen is a wonderful reminder to all of us, including myself, to be grateful and to make the most of our abilities. If Owen can persevere, I can too. He has no idea how much he has impacted my life.

We are taught to be grateful for things in life when we are young. But as we get older and busier with life, we frequently let the idea of being grateful go as we take on additional responsibilities.

Here are my favorite ways of expanding our ability to be more grateful:

1. Read and learn from people who have overcome obstacles and adversity.
2. Travel. Some people are in more difficult positions than you are, far more difficult than you could ever

fathom. Sometimes you may not even need to travel that far.
3. Converse with first responders and nurses who are willing to share about their life. You may hear unreal stories that make you appreciate the littlest of things.
4. Reflect on a memorial (celebration of life) of a family member or close friend who you loved and admired. Think back on how they lived and what they went through.

In general, if you are a hunter who is grateful for what hunting has brought you and are not sure what you would do without it, improving *Your Hunting Healthspan* would ensure your best chance to keep being involved in this lifestyle with fewer health limitations.

FAITH

I believe having trust in a certain belief has the power to change the trajectory of our lives completely. A person could be at their lowest point in life and still be able to climb out using the strong ropes of faith. On the other hand, someone could be in a good place in their life and discover that faith was what they needed to help them realize the important aspects of life they had been overlooking. Faith has shifted my perspective—to look beyond my needs and focus on something much greater. It's helped refine what I truly value in this life, how I want to spend my time, and gratitude for everything in between. Here is my personal experience of how much faith has enhanced my quality of life and well-being.

Growing up, I didn't practice any particular faith or belief. When I was a child, I used to pray, but it was only when I wanted something. I wasn't really introduced to Christianity until my wife and

I started dating. I was initially skeptical, but as time passed, I grew more receptive and open-minded, which allowed me to have several profound internal epiphanies. I have no doubt been able to explore deeper layers of myself in regard to my thoughts, surroundings, and existence as a result of immersing myself in the spiritual aspect of life through faith.

Nowadays, I read scripture verses while eating my first meal of the day. I've come to love this new habit that I've developed genuinely. I've discovered that this is a fantastic time to really internalize the verse's main idea and to reflect back on and examine my own life to see how and when I might put it into practice. When I was younger, I recall talking with my uncle Linden about scripture. I didn't understand at the time why he claimed that after becoming paralyzed, scripture and faith literally saved his life. I'm starting to see what he meant by its impact now. Scripture can be especially useful in equipping us with the skills we need to deal with challenging situations and times. After a tragedy, we could occasionally feel depressed or like life is in a bad position. Whatever our circumstances, faith of any kind can give us the strength we need to overcome anything.

As my journey with faith and personal development has grown, I have also put more effort into prayer. Every day before my first meal, I give all my focus to expressing my personal prayer, which expresses how I truly feel. It sounds like this:

"Thank you for my relationship with my beautiful wife. Thank you for my growing healthy boy. Thank you for the ability to see, think, feel, move, speak, and remember. Thank you for keeping my family safe. Thank you for the roof over our heads. Thank you for this meal. Thank you for helping me find the causes of my ignorance. Thank you, God, for another day on this planet."

This prayer has given me a firm platform on which to face life's successes or failures, and it has allowed me to feel more sincere gratitude and inner peace. The cool thing about prayers, in my opinion, is that they can be whatever the person wants them to be. For instance, my prayer is similar to yet distinct from what I say immediately following the harvest of wild game. When there is flexibility in how we can compose our prayers, beautiful things can occur, such as inner peace. Something that, when experienced, can alter how we view life.

There are many diverse faiths one can believe in and practice, which is one of the many wonderful things about it. The fact that there are different races, cultures, customs, and other characteristics among the people of this planet implies that each of us has the opportunity to find and choose the faith that best serves our lives. Since each faith has its own traits and tenets, people can choose the route that suits them best.

For instance, I have incorporated numerous Buddhist and Confucian principles into my life. And even though my understanding of these other faiths is rudimentary, they have still, in some small way, improved the quality of my life. Learning about different faiths may seem like an unusual path, but for me, it has made a significant difference in how I view and live life.

In the grand scheme of things, other people's beliefs don't really matter as long as they do good. Consider it. Would you want someone else to experience positive benefits and a better quality of life from trusting in a particular faith? It may not matter what faith people trust and believe in because their life is better lived with it. I really believe that it is possible to disagree, be polite, get past indifference, and accept one another's preferences without giving in to arguments or internal anger. Perhaps there are numerous paths leading to the truth and destination we all desire.

What I've learned is that having faith can help you in a lot of different areas of life, including our ability to handle adversity storms more effectively when they arise. The key word here is when, for each of us will experience adversity in the form of hardship, struggle, and hopelessness to varied degrees at some point or points in our lives.

With my little experience, I have discovered that there is no end to what one can gain from faith. The following are the benefits I've experienced as a result of my scripture study:

- Heightened clarity
- Gratitude
- Less bitterness
- Open mind
- At ease
- Humility
- Tolerance
- Liberation
- Calmness
- Happier
- Emotionally grounded
- Stronger "will"

In the end, think about looking into different faiths and philosophical perspectives to see if anything appeals to you for your unique needs. Whatever you choose, when you fully immerse yourself and allow yourself to be opened to something bigger, it may provide you the opportunity to grow individually, enhance your mental and spiritual health, and it may even significantly change the direction of your life.

AGING IS A PRIVILEGE

Let's start developing the mindset that aging is a privilege; we only get one life. Start by recalling instances where things may have turned out differently, and you might not be alive today. I know I can. I remember several times coming dangerously close to drowning and nearly driving off a cliff while deer hunting. I also recall renting an apartment where the house above me had been the location of numerous murder attempts. According to the local sheriff who spoke with me during their investigation, I was lucky not to become a victim.

Many of you probably have scenarios in mind that are much worse than mine. The point is that the amount of life that occurs is not guaranteed for any of us, no matter our age, so make the best of your time while you can.

I've attended a lot of memorial services for friends and family members, and many of them weren't just because of poor health but also for unexpected reasons. Some of these people loved hunting. When we reflect and allow ourselves to be vulnerable to the circumstance, these moments of sorrow over losing loved ones can really build our spirit. I believe that we owe it to these people to live to the fullest extent of our capabilities and to make them proud. They would probably want us to do that, in my opinion.

All we can do is keep moving forward and have a better understanding of how quickly this life game passes by, turning each of us into a mere memory. Let's start focusing our "will" on what we can do right now to enhance our health rather than on the past that we would like to change. To experience what it's like to be bursting with energy, joy, and life, we owe it to ourselves to improve our current health status. Life seems more worthwhile when you realize how amazing this body, mind, and spirit can feel.

Interestingly, several medical professionals have noted that those with a positive outlook on aging may live many more years of good health than those who don't (attitude matters). Yes, that includes letting go of our anger toward our facial wrinkles or gray hair—some people never get to experience this. Make a conscious effort to combat these thoughts with acceptance and honor because aging is a natural part of life. Embrace aging while also finding ways to age better. It's possible to be older but not feel older.

Humans, compared to other living things on this planet, have the opportunity to experience life in incredibly detailed ways because of our exceptional physical and mental capacities. We are lucky to be born into a human body. Given that being a human is a gift, aging is also something to be grateful for and, depending on how you view it, may impact *Your Hunting Healthspan*.

PRIORITIZE YOURSELF

One of the lessons we learn early in life is that being selfish is a negative quality. This seems like a valid remark to make about many things in life. In my experience, this notion can, however, change depending on the context. In my opinion, being selfish when it comes to our health is a good thing. What I'm trying to express is that I think it's important to prioritize taking care of ourselves before helping others. Does this indicate that we should never help those in need? Absolutely not. It's all about *balance*. Helping others is wonderful, and I strongly encourage you to keep doing it. However, if we put all of our efforts into helping others, we may find that other facets of our lives start to fall out of balance, including our health. I believe that prioritizing our health by adopting healthier lifestyle choices could be prudent. Because let's face it, we literally do not exist without our health.

Our health may start to deteriorate when we put off taking care of our needs because we are busy with those of others. If this occurs frequently, health limitations can develop sooner. As a result, it will be harder to satisfy other people's needs, and our existence on earth is now in danger.

Unfortunately, working nurses today still have a lot to overcome in this regard. Despite the fact that it is their occupation, nurses periodically need to put their needs on a pedestal and exercise selfishness in order to maintain their physical and mental well-being. If they don't, they may not only be unable to provide the care they need due to their own poor health, but they may also put their lives at risk of developing chronic diseases and other health problems. The attitude of being selfish in addressing our needs, especially our health, does not require us to be a nurse. Anyone can do it, which is why it's in this book.

The idea that we should try to help others in order to divert our focus from our own problems comes to mind when we are selfish for our own needs. Helping others is rewarding and increases our self-esteem. Helping ourselves requires work and effort in areas we might not want to tackle, which is why some aspects of our lives never improve. When we spend the bulk of our time and energy taking care of others to ignore our own needs, such as our health purposely, life may seem fairly challenging at times. As a result, we experience a sense of being overwhelmed, stressed out, and in the grip of anxiety. We may never be able to change our lives if we avoid doing things that we know need to be done to make them better.

A long-term plan for leading a balanced existence is not to spend all our time trying to please or help others while never taking the time to focus on ourselves. Helping others is admirable, but we might want to reconsider when it becomes a distraction from our own lives. To enhance life and health, we will eventually need to take care of our own needs. That is if we want life to be better.

Today, change something. Choose an area of your life that calls for improvement. Make the required efforts to improve it. This demonstrates that you are putting more effort into improving your life. When your life has improved, think about helping others while beginning to work toward your next goal. It will feel wonderful to let go of the stress, anxiety, and tension that has accumulated in your body and mind as a result of avoidance. You will experience this relief if you *prioritize yourself*.

THE CHOICE IS YOURS

When I say that I wish I could control your daily efforts and habits, I really mean it. I wish I could make you choose better lifestyle choices, but I'm afraid I can't. I wish I could put a tiny robot inside your head to advise you to lead a healthier lifestyle. I wish I could take your hunting gear away from you until you lower your blood pressure or lose weight. I wish I could summon your thumb to stop scrolling on social media for hours watching other people live their lives so you could work toward your goals. I wish I could pull you up off the couch from watching TV and get you moving. I wish I could cast a spell on you to put down that snack. All of these examples are not possible because, in real life, the choice to live a healthier lifestyle is *yours*, not mine.

I can't reverse your type 2 diabetes. But you can even though you might have been told that "Your health is just how it is, and you are stuck with type 2 diabetes." If you choose to, you might be able to reverse your type 2 diabetes by making better dietary choices, such as eating more nourishing foods, trying the 16:8 method, and snacking less. If you become aware of this and take action, the somewhat terrifying long-term consequences, such as heart disease, stroke, vision problems, amputations, and kidney disease, may be lessened. All of which can lead to fewer hunting opportunities. You can take action to prevent these health limitations if you want.

The same is true with depression. The truth is, whether you take medication or not, there are many things you can do to better your situation. Making better lifestyle choices, such as consistently working out, eating nourishing foods, spending time outdoors and in natural light, taking breaks from social media, challenging yourself, avoiding negative influences like bad music and people, creating something like art, getting enough sleep, and surrounding yourself with supportive people. These are the kinds of habits that can offer you a fighting chance against those demonic thoughts. This is particularly relevant for me because I think I had a mild case at the time my father passed away, though I was unaware of it. I was also unaware at the time of how improving my lifestyle choices could have a significant influence on my mental health, improve my mood, and set me up for success. There are things you can do to improve your situation, but the choice is ultimately up to you.

Once you realize that the change you need to make is something you already have within, you will realize that you are completely in charge of yourself. Anytime we place the blame for our health on our boss, society, the healthcare system, our significant other, our children, or anything else we can think of, we begin to feel powerless and victimized. Our future is now in the hands of another.

When we are having trouble with anything, it's a challenge, or we are not getting the results we desire, it is fairly easy to complain, make excuses, and rationalize things. From the outside, it makes us feel better, but on the inside, it's a slow way for us to torture ourselves. I used to make excuses all the time. We can justify all we want to till we are blue in the face. The thing is, it usually doesn't change anything. Even others might try to make excuses for you. For instance, many parents warned me that after my wife and I welcomed a child, I wouldn't be able to continue training consistently. The ironic thing is that in addition to training every day, I am also training harder than I ever have. I almost believed the excuse they made for me until I didn't.

Making fewer excuses and better lifestyle choices means you raise the odds of making additional positive choices. It's a push of the lined-up dominoes. Making one healthy lifestyle choice, like going to bed earlier, often leads to another, like choosing higher-quality foods. We can prevent distractions, multitasking, forgetfulness, and ineffective time management by keeping track of weekly responsibilities on a calendar. This gives us more time to stretch, read, and shoot our bow. However, the domino line shows the reverse to be true. Staying up late and neglecting sleep raises the likelihood of expressing a weakened moral compass and poor character traits the following day. Sitting on the couch excessively raises the likelihood of becoming very stiff and weak and potentially straining muscles while performing daily tasks.

I propose that you make better lifestyle choices to change yourself into someone you can be proud of. Not just apply effort for the next three months after reading this book while you are pumped up. I'm talking about consistent effort for the rest of your life, especially if you want the health you have never had. This seems like a better plan and way of life to me than hoping for something to get better.

Hoping for something to get better and achieve our goals, without applying effort, won't get us closer to where we want to be. In fact, next time you have a free weekend, I want you to head to a location on earth that contains hundreds to thousands of goals. It's called the local cemetery. Look around you and realize that many of the individuals who are currently with Mother Earth had many goals they were never able to achieve. Goals like enhancing their health and well-being to live better quality lives. Many weren't successful because they waited for something to change for them. No action was ever taken, only words that expressed that they wanted to achieve something.

Let's be honest and accountable with ourselves regarding our goals. Either we "actually" want them or we "kind of" want them. There is a big difference. To put it another way, those who "actually" want to achieve goals will work diligently toward them, no matter how long it takes. As you read this, begin working toward your goal(s) if you actually want to accomplish them. Like right this very moment.

Here Is a Simple Template for Achieving a Goal

STEP 1: Pick something you want to accomplish, individually speaking.

STEP 2: Write it on something that you can see every day. Maybe a calendar, on your fridge, phone screen saver, etc.

STEP 3: Educate yourself on finding ways that you can accomplish this goal.

STEP 4: Employ action and effort every single day to some degree using what you have learned.

STEP 5: Be consistent with your effort no matter how long it takes to accomplish your goal.

If you follow this template and use it for each goal, you have a better chance of succeeding, especially if you are patient, persistent, and remember your reason (your "why"). If you have a compelling "why" to serve as a continual reminder of your goals, it will be much easier to progress toward them every day, regardless of what happens.

> One step forward today toward your goals is one less step you need to take tomorrow.

We must understand that until we employ action, no amount of seminars, books, magazines, online courses, therapists, social media posts, videos, or podcasts about how to improve our well-being will be helpful. Put some effort into taking that first step (initial action). Then take another step. Then, another step. Continue with your steps (be consistent) and watch what happens to your life.

Make your bed, shoot your bow, perform pushups or squats at home, go scouting, clean the dishes, go on dates with your significant other, read books, do laundry and fold clothes, clean the garage, watch less TV, list daily duties on a calendar, go to bed earlier, stretch, and take a cold shower. These are all excellent choices for taking the initial step. You are capable; take charge and move forward. Good things start with one step in the right direction.

After we rewire our brains, put all our thoughts, feelings, and energy into improving our health and take action, our ability to create the life we want starts to take shape. If we are willing to put in the effort, we can improve ourselves every day of this life. Make an effort to improve your health so that you can go on more hunting trips, spend more time with your family, and thoroughly enjoy life. It's time to revamp your way of life right now so you can look back on it without regret. The choice is always and forever *yours*.

THE MOVEMENT

My hope is that you invest time in learning how to age better and prevent disease without relying solely on my ideas and this mere book. This book is not the supreme authority nor the standard. It's nothing more than a collection of concepts, ideas, and thoughts—a possible direction and nothing more. Through independent inquiry, you can delve much deeper into each strategy and create your own plan for aging better and preventing disease.

Make time to think independently, explore, critically evaluate, and put into practice everything that seems to have potential value; disregard the rest. The opportunity to start a new life has arrived. Not on the first of the month, the first Monday of the following week, or the first day of the new year. At this precise moment. The time to join the *movement* is right now.

In the movement, hunters from all over the world are beginning to make better lifestyle choices consistently in order to experience more opening days and hunting opportunities. Since I began writing this book, this is what I have imagined it to look like. Yes, choosing a healthy lifestyle can occasionally be difficult. You will struggle and experience a sense of uncertainty like a windstorm. It could seem like it's taking a while to reach your goals and get the outcomes you want. Continue on; you will feel proud of yourself if you do. Progress over perfection means the effort will always be rewarding and give you a better chance to hunt more.

If you keep in mind the type of health you desire and the kind of person you want to become, anything is possible if you persevere. There are no shortcuts to making a significant change in your life. Whatever the reason, if you are unhappy or dissatisfied with your health or life, realize that you can change it. We can all make improvements to our physical, mental, and spiritual health, no matter our current position. Believe me when I tell you that if you make one lifestyle choice that is advantageous to your health, your entire experience of life could change.

Being a part of this movement also requires thinking beyond ourselves. Wouldn't it be great to set up the next generation of hunters for success? We can do that by directly improving our health so that we can remain in their lives for longer and continue to be positive role models who can inspire, educate, and mentor. Keeping this way of life alive and setting better examples for the next generation of hunters depends on us improving our health and passing this knowledge on. The key is to make sure we are following our own advice and living it.

Pay it forward and educate the next generation of hunters on these health-promoting strategies to set them up for success. If they learned that better health enables them to spend more time with their family, engage in activities they enjoy, and go hunting more, that would be wonderful. The next generation of hunters needs healthy, humble, and positive role models more than ever. You could be that person. I hope to be one of those individuals for many years to come.

You might know what you want to work on first now that you've finished the book. Great, let's press onward. Find a partner in this journey toward improved lifestyle choices if you can. Set some goals, support one another, get feedback, be honest and accountable to one another, and overcome any obstacles. If you don't know where to start, read the section, Call to Action that follows the Conclusion because it provides extra guidance.

I hope those in the hunting community enjoy a long, healthy life filled with plenty of opening days and hunting opportunities. Long live our way of life and those who contribute to it. As for myself, I'll do my best and keep treating every day as a chance to enhance these health-promoting strategies and embrace fresh concepts to become the best version of myself. I have much more to give back to the hunting community. I'm just getting started.

Remember: without health, there is no more hunting.

Ways #65–73 to Age Better and Prevent Disease

65. Enjoy the process of improving your health, not just the result.

66. Remember: obstacles, failures, mistakes, and losses are disguised as learning opportunities.

67. Be willing to modify your perspective on all things continually.

68. Use your passion to help and inspire others or the journey of life itself as a purpose.

69. Keep pushing yourself toward your goals. There is no limit to your potential.

70. Practice gratitude.

71. Explore different faiths.

72. Prioritize yourself.

73. Continue finding more ways to elevate your physical, mental, and spiritual health.

CONCLUSION

Without health, we won't be able to hunt and do things we love; we won't have a schedule, family time, retirement, or the ability to support conservation initiatives. The time to change is now if you want to get healthier. Not tomorrow, not next Monday, or the beginning of the month. Exactly as you read these lines right now. Experiment with these strategies if you want to feel good, strengthen your immune system, live life the way you want, age better, prevent disease, hunt more with fewer health limitations, and improve *Your Hunting Healthspan*:

1. Adopt the prevention mindset for health.
2. Look at chronic stressors as an opportunity to learn something new and realize they are insignificant in the grand scheme of the universe.
3. Be more optimistic.
4. Minimize complaining.
5. Display more kindness.
6. Show more humility.
7. Control and minimize your reactive ego and pride.

8. Be fully accountable for everything you say and do. Apologize when wrong.
9. Be more honest.
10. Be more respectful to people and the environment.
11. Listen with intent and avoid "blind listening."
12. Be more present with your body and mind.
13. Employ more self-awareness regarding your thoughts, emotions, and actions.
14. Put your mindset in neutral.
15. Provide support and love to your family and friends.
16. Love your significant other not because you have to but because you get to.
17. Establish your purpose-driven reason for consistent training.
18. Improve your foot speed, grip strength, aerobic capacity, midline support, leg strength, and rotator cuff stability through different movements.
19. Improve your biomechanics and posture to minimize injuries and range-of-motion restrictions.
20. Static stretch to some degree every day.
21. Incorporate mobility practices for injury prevention.
22. Use heat and movement (specific to the athletic injury) to increase blood flow and assist with recovery. Use ice to block unmanageable pain.
23. Consume a variety of nourishing foods based on your individual needs.
24. Eat till you are content, not stuffed.

25. Incorporate a treat allowance to maintain balance for your specific needs.
26. Be consistent (patient) and accountable (honest) with your dietary habits.
27. Aim for drinking filtered water based on thirst or half your body weight in ounces.
28. Incorporate unrefined salt into your meals and your water.
29. Incorporate the 16:8 method.
30. Minimize snacking and eat less often.
31. Incorporate dietary supplements for your individual needs.
32. Explore blood, saliva, stool, and gene tests.
33. Go to bed and wake up close to the same time every day.
34. Have a screen curfew before bed and when you wake up.
35. Switch your phone and computer screen to red light/warmer colors.
36. Be done eating at least two hours before bed.
37. Get outside for natural light exposure first thing in the morning, during midday, and before dark.
38. Wait a few hours after waking before ingesting caffeine.
39. Aim for seven to nine hours of good quality sleep.
40. Develop code words or numbers to use for anxiety.
41. Incorporate nasal breathing before/during/after training, while hunting, before you sleep, when you want to recenter yourself, etc.
42. Incorporate more stillness (daily/weekly/monthly) in natural settings.

43. Build up your "will" by being more self-disciplined.
44. Practice grounding (direct skin contact with soil, sand, grass, etc.).
45. Get your gardening on.
46. Immerse yourself in nature and to more anions (rivers, forests, waterfalls, mountains, oceans, etc.).
47. Obtain more sunlight exposure in doses according to your skin tone.
48. Modify your environment by bringing plants into your residence and/or work.
49. Surround your water with positive sounds and words.
50. Incorporate sauna use.
51. Incorporate cold-water immersion.
52. Always and forever be a student for life and aim for more clarity.
53. Read more books.
54. Get your chess game on.
55. Explore methods of making music.
56. Cultivate visual art to express yourself and your thoughts.
57. Partake in a backup hobby or hobbies.
58. Adopt and incorporate less is more (minimalism) into all areas of life.
59. Reestablish a new relationship with time.
60. Avoid putting yourself in positions of regret; apply consistent effort into all things.

61. Seek challenging tasks regularly to experience more of life.
62. Be more authentic and focus on yourself, not others' opinions.
63. Find mentors who can give you advice, support, and guidance.
64. Embrace wholeness.
65. Enjoy the process of improving your health, not just the result.
66. Remember: obstacles, failures, mistakes, and losses are disguised as learning opportunities.
67. Be willing to modify your perspective on all things continually.
68. Use your passion to help and inspire others or the journey of life itself as a purpose.
69. Keep pushing yourself toward your goals; there is no limit to your potential.
70. Practice gratitude.
71. Explore different faiths.
72. Prioritize yourself.
73. Continue finding more ways to elevate your physical, mental, and spiritual health.

CALL TO ACTION

HOW DO WE START INCORPORATING BETTER LIFESTYLE CHOICES?

Now that you have finished reading the 73 *ways* that can help us age better and prevent disease, the next step is to *act*. When we begin to consider the areas of our health and lives that we wish to improve, at times, it can feel overwhelming. Keep it simple and remind yourself why you are making changes. Then, consider using one of the options below as a means of action:

1. Pick one or two strategies to improve each month. Select new ones to resume the cycle after you feel they have improved and are still improving. Tell your hunting buddies, friends, family, and coworkers about the improvements you're making, and encourage them to follow your example.
2. Find a friend who will be your teammate. Incorporate as many of the health-promoting strategies detailed in this book on a regular basis as you can as a team for a full year. Every daily lifestyle choice (strategy) counts for one point. Document everything you and your teammate do for your health in writing, audio, or video, along with

your current point total. Find another team to compete with and spread the word about it. Share and connect with others on social media about how you are putting in the effort to improve *Your Hunting Healthspan* (Use hashtag: #yourhuntinghealthspan).
3. For guidance on where to start for your specific needs and extra resources via articles, videos, and podcasts, go to http://camoandwind.com/.

ACKNOWLEDGMENTS

JON LOREN, thank you for introducing me to such a meaningful and worthwhile lifestyle. I hope you enjoy this book and everything it stands for, and I look forward to hunting with you again someday.

Jan Loren, thank you for providing me with the best life a son could hope for. I will always be grateful for all that you have done and are still doing for me.

Rylee Loren, thank you for your love and support. None of this would have been possible without you. I can't express how thankful I am for you on so many levels. The best and luckiest thing that has ever happened to me is you, and it always will be.

Declan Loren, a.k.a. "monster man." You don't understand it yet, but you are the center of your mother and my greatest love. Thank you for allowing us to experience one of the most joyful experiences a person can have—becoming parents. I hope you see how beautiful this life can be.

Nathan Loren, thank you for pulling me out of the college slump and encouraging me to work out. Because of you, my life's trajectory was radically altered.

Erek Loren, thank you for your effort in getting the family together to spend time together. It means more than you know. Family over everything.

Linden Loren (uncle), thank you for being inspirational beyond belief. May your positive attitude spread through me and others for eternity.

Margo Dutton and Lynda Pritchett, thank you for being the best aunts I could ever ask for. My childhood was highly joyous because of you two.

Jay Burkey, thank you for the mentoring, inspiration, and life lessons that you have provided for me. I hope you're enjoying your time in Hawaii.

Ray Benner, thank you for being a great father figure to me. I hope to emulate you as I age. Let's keep it going.

Pat and Vonda Van Rooyen, thank you for providing resources and helping me cultivate ANION. None of this would be possible without you guys believing in me.

Mr. Fulton, thank you for mentoring me in seventh grade on all things life. Those moments meant more than you think.

Coach Axel, thank you for encouraging me to step on that bus to Ensenada, Mexico for the mission trip. This experience was one of the most impactful; I vividly remember it to this day.

The people who helped me on my training journey: Deana Wyland, Joey Dussel, Mike Johnson, James Alexzander, and Adam Neiffer. Thank you all!

The people who helped me on my teaching and coaching journey: Joe Meekins, Jessica Smith, Micah Smith, Brian Mehl, Kerri Lemerande, Casey Horn, Todd Zimmermann, Cole Pouliot, and Susie Orsborn. Thank you so much!

Andy Evans, thank you for your guidance on how to integrate business with hunting effectively. I am appreciative of those conversations.

Seth Bovio, thank you for your encouragement to keep pushing forward no matter how many failures I experience. People like you give people like me hope to build a business to support a family.

Sijo Adriano D. Emperado, thank you for being a part of my family. I am honored to have been named after you. Long live your power and positive influence on others.

Owen Robinson, thank you for exposing me to new perspectives. I will make the most out of this life for you. You are the strongest individual I have ever met.

Larry and Dolly Kammer, thank you for joining our family and letting us be a part of your journey.

Wetmores and Cottermans, thank you for welcoming me into your family and being supportive of everything I do. I couldn't ask for better in-laws.

Close friends and hunting buddies, thank you all for being a part of my journey. I'm grateful to have such wonderful friends!

Bruce Lee, thank you for your philosophical work that has allowed me to rewire my brain toward liberation and living simply. I hope someday I will be able to join in the conversations with Tony Ramos, my father, and you. May your lessons forever travel through time.

Mother Nature, thank you for everything you are and everything you provide me. Keep making me humbled and teaching me new perspectives.

Indirect support from companies and people (First Lite, Howl for Wildlife, Concept 2, Sorinex Outdoors, Ben Patrick, *Bear Hunting Magazine*, Celtic Sea Salt, Redmond Real Salt, Carnivore Aurelius, Kudupoint, Kifaru, PLUNGE, StHealthy Hunter, and Spartan Precision). Thank you for allowing me to share your product and work with the hunting community.

Direct support from Jim Shockey, Kenton Carruth, Jana Waller, Rob Gearing, Sereena Thompson, Aron Snyder, Tom Ryle, Bert Sorin, and Travis Glassman, I can't thank you enough for seeing the value in this book for how it can positively contribute to the hunting community. May your years be filled with robust health and many hunting opportunities.

A huge thanks to my entire team at Scribe Media. My publishing managers Aleza D'Agostino, Esty Pittman, and Joy Yeou. My book layout designer, Lawna Oldfield. Erin Sky, my marketing copywriter, Rikki Jump, my marketing manager, Michael Nagin, my book cover designer, Hal Clifford, my editor-in-chief, and Nicole Jobe and Alan Gintzler my editors. I can't thank you, guys, enough for your support in helping me bring my ideas to life!

ENDNOTES

1. Preetha Anand et al., "Cancer Is a Preventable Disease That Requires Major Lifestyle Changes," *Pharmaceutical Research* 25, no. 9 (September 2008): 2097–2116, https://doi.org/10.1007/s11095-008-9661-9.

2. Ai Ikeda et al., "Pessimistic Orientation in Relation to Telomere Length in Older Men: The VA Normative Aging Study," *Psychoneuroendocrinology* 42 (April 2014): 68–76, https://doi.org/10.1016/j.psyneuen.2014.01.001; Lewina O. Lee et al., "Optimism Is Associated with Exceptional Longevity in 2 Epidemiologic Cohorts of Men and Women," *Proceedings of the National Academy of Sciences of the United States of America* 116, no. 37 (September 2019): 18357–18362, https://doi.org/10.1073/pnas.1900712116.

3. Keiko Otake et al., "Happy People Become Happier through Kindness: A Counting Kindnesses Intervention," *Journal of Happiness Studies* 7, no. 3 (September 2006): 361–375, https://doi.org/10.1007/s10902-005-3650-z.

4. Daisy Fancourt and Andrew Steptoe, "Television Viewing and Cognitive Decline in Older Age: Findings from the English Longitudinal Study of Ageing," *Scientific Reports* 9, no. 1 (February 2019): 2851, https://doi.org/10.1038/s41598-019-39354-4.

5. Larry A. Tucker, "Physical Activity and Telomere Length in U.S. Men and Women: An NHANES Investigation," *Preventative Medicine* 100 (July 2017): 145–151, https://doi.org/10.1016/j.ypmed.2017.04.027.

6. Gabe Mirkin, "Why Ice Delays Recovery," DrMirkin.com, September 16, 2015, https://www.drmirkin.com/fitness/why-ice-delays-recovery.html.

7. Mirkin, "Why Ice Delays Recovery."

8. Chris Kresser, "How Industrial Seed Oils Are Making Us Sick," ChrisKresser.com, February 19, 2019, https://chriskresser.com/how-industrial-seed-oils-are-making-us-sick/.

9. Eveline Deloose et al., "The Migrating Motor Complex: Control Mechanisms and Its Role in Health and Disease," *Nature Reviews: Gastroenterology and Hepatology* 9, no. 5 (March 2012): 271–285, https://doi.org/10.1038/nrgastro.2012.57.

10 Alex Formuzis, "Roundup for Breakfast, Part 2: In New Tests, Weed Killer Found in All Kids' Cereals Sampled," Environmental Working Group, October 24, 2018, https://www.ewg.org/news-insights/news-release/2018/10/roundup-breakfast-part-2-new-tests-weed-killer-found-all-kids.

11 Carla S. Möller-Levet et al., "Effects of Insufficient Sleep on Circadian Rhythmicity and Expression Amplitude of the Human Blood Transcriptome," *Proceedings of the National Academy of Sciences of the United States of America* 110, no. 12 (February 2013): E1132–E1141, https://doi.org/10.1073/pnas.1217154110.

12 Angela J. Beck, "Rotating Night Shift Work Can Be Hazardous to Your Health," Elsevier, January 5, 2015, https://www.elsevier.com/about/press-releases/research-and-journals/rotating-night-shift-work-can-be-hazardous-to-your-health.

13 Maria Basta et al., "Chronic Insomnia and the Stress System," *Sleep Medicine Clinics* 2, no. 2 (June 2007): 279–291, https://doi.org/10.1016/j.jsmc.2007.04.002.

14 Yasmin Anwar, "Stressed to the Max? Deep Sleep Can Rewire the Anxious Brain," Berkeley News, November 4, 2019, https://news.berkeley.edu/2019/11/04/deep-sleep-can-rewire-the-anxious-brain/.

15 Satchin Panda, "Early Time-Restricted Feeding for the Prevention of Diabetes," *My Circadian Clock* (blog), accessed February 28, 2023, https://blog.mycircadianclock.org/light-therapeutics-how-light-or-darkness-affects-our-circadian-clock-sleep-and-mood/.

16 Manolis Kogevinas et al., "Effect of Mistimed Eating Patterns on Breast and Prostate Cancer Risk (MCC–Spain Study)," *International Journal of Cancer* 143, no. 10 (November 2018): 2380–2389, https://doi.org/10.1002/ijc.31649.

17 Patricia J. Murphy et al., "Nonsteroidal Anti-Inflammatory Drugs Affect Normal Sleep Patterns in Humans," *Physiology & Behavior* 55, no. 6 (June 1994): 1063–1066, https://doi.org/10.1016/0031-9384(94)90388-3.

18 Danielle Pacheco, "Drowsy Driving vs. Drunk Driving: How Similar Are They?," Sleep Foundation, last modified June 24, 2022, https://www.sleepfoundation.org/drowsy-driving/drowsy-driving-vs-drunk-driving.

19 Michael D. Stein and Peter D. Friedmann, "Disturbed Sleep and Its Relationship to Alcohol Use," *Substance Abuse* 26, no. 1 (2006): 1–13, https://doi.org/10.1300/J465v26n01_01.

20 Darija Baković et al., "Effect of Human Splenic Contraction on Variation in Circulating Blood Cell Counts," *Clinical and Experimental Pharmacology and Physiology* 32, no. 11 (November 2005): 944–951, https://doi.org/10.1111/j.1440-1681.2005.04289.x; Darija Baković et al., "Spleen Volume and Blood Flow Response to Repeated Breath-Hold Apneas," *Journal of Applied Physiology* 95, no. 4 (October 2003): 1460–1466, https://doi.org/10.1152/japplphysiol.00221.2003.

21 Britta K. Hölzel et al., "Mindfulness Practice Leads to Increases in Regional Brain Gray Matter Density," *Psychiatry Research: Neuroimaging* 191, no. 1 (January 2011): 36–43, https://doi.org/10.1016/j.pscychresns.2010.08.006.

22 Mel Robbins, "How to Stop Screwing Yourself Over," filmed June 2011 at TEDx San Francisco, uploaded June 11, 2011, YouTube video, 21:39, https://www.youtube.com/watch?v=Lp7E973zozc.

23 James L. Oschman, Gaétan Chevalier, and Richard Brown, "The Effects of Grounding (Earthing) on Inflammation, the Immune Response, Wound Healing, and Prevention and Treatment of Chronic Inflammatory and Autoimmune Diseases," *Journal of Inflammation Research* 2015, no. 8 (March 2015): 83–96, https://doi.org/10.2147/JIR.S69656.

24 Gaétan Chevalier et al., "Earthing (Grounding) the Human Body Reduces Blood Viscosity—A Major Factor in Cardiovascular Disease," *The Journal of Alternative and Complementary Medicine* 19, no. 2 (February 2013): 102–110, https://doi.org/10.1089/acm.2011.0820.

25 Gaétan Chevalier et al., "The Effects of Grounding (Earthing) on Bodyworkers' Pain and Overall Quality of Life: A Randomized Controlled Trial," *Explore* 15, no. 3 (May–June 2019): 181–190, https://doi.org/10.1016/j.explore.2018.10.001; Gaétan Chevalier, "The Effect of Grounding the Human Body on Mood," *Psychological Reports* 116, no. 2 (April 2015): 534–542, https://doi.org/10.2466/06.PR0.116k21w5; Maurice Ghaly and Dale Teplitz, "The Biologic Effects of Grounding the Human Body during Sleep as Measured by Cortisol Levels and Subjective Reporting of Sleep, Pain, and Stress," *The Journal of Alternative and Complementary Medicine* 10, no. 5 (October 2004): 767–776, https://doi.org/10.1089/acm.2004.10.767.

26 Christopher McDougall, "The Barefoot Running Debate," ChrisMcDougall.com, accessed February 28, 2023, https://www.chrismcdougall.com/born-to-run/the-barefoot-running-debate/.

27 Carnivore Aurelius, "Veganism Kills More Animals than the Carnivore Diet," CarnivoreAurelius.com, March 4, 2020, https://carnivoreaurelius.com/veganism-kills/.

28 Masashi Soga, Kevin J. Gaston, and Yuichi Yamaura, "Gardening Is Beneficial for Health: A Meta-Analysis," *Preventative Medicine Reports* 5 (March 2017): 92–99, https://doi.org/10.1016/j.pmedr.2016.11.007.

29 Sin-Ae Park et al., "Benefits of Gardening Activities for Cognitive Function according to Measurement of Brain Nerve Growth Factor Levels," *International Journal of Environmental Research and Public Health* 16, no. 5 (March 2019): 760, https://doi.org/10.3390/ijerph16050760.

30 Neil E. Klepeis et al., "The National Human Activity Pattern Survey (NHAPS): A Resource for Assessing Exposure to Environmental Pollutants," *Journal of*

Exposure Science and Environmental Epidemiology 11, no. 3 (2001): 231–252, https://doi.org/10.1038/sj.jea.7500165.

31 "Volatile Organic Compounds in Your Home," Minnesota Department of Health, last modified October 20, 2022, https://www.health.state.mn.us/communities/environment/air/toxins/voc.htm.

32 Rona Cherry, "The Surprising Health Benefits of Indoor Plants," NYCity Woman, accessed February 28, 2023, https://www.nycitywoman.com/the-surprising-health-benefits-of-indoor-plants/.

33 Craig Gustafson, "Bruce Ames, PhD, and Rhonda Patrick, PhD: Discussing the Triage Concept and the Vitamin D–Serotonin Connection," *Integrative Medicine* 13, no. 6 (December 2014): 34–42, https://www.ncbi.nlm.nih.gov/pmc/articles/PMC4566436/pdf/34-42.pdf.

34 Harvard University: T. H. Chan School of Public Health, "Vitamin D," *The Nutrition Source*, last modified November 2022, https://www.hsph.harvard.edu/nutritionsource/vitamin-d/; Mina Bashir et al., "Effects of High Doses of Vitamin D3 on Mucosa-Associated Gut Microbiome Vary between Regions of the Human Gastrointestinal Tract," *European Journal of Nutrition* 55, no. 4 (2016): 1479–1489, https://doi.org/10.1007/s00394-015-0966-2; Giovanna Muscogiuri et al., "The Lullaby of the Sun: The Role of Vitamin D in Sleep Disturbance," *Sleep Medicine* 54 (February 2019): 262–265, https://doi.org/10.1016/j.sleep.2018.10.033.

35 Chris Kresser, "Tips for a Healthy Summer: Part 1," ChrisKresser.com, June 29, 2012, https://chriskresser.com/tips-for-a-healthy-summer-part-1/.

36 "Unhealthiest States for Skin Cancer Risk May Surprise You," *City of Hope* (blog), May 24, 2016, https://www.cancercenter.com/community/blog/2016/05/unhealthiest-states-for-skin-cancer-risk-may-surprise-you.

37 Tanjaniina Laukkanen et al., "Sauna Bathing Is Associated with Reduced Cardiovascular Mortality and Improves Risk Prediction in Men and Women: A Prospective Cohort Study," *BMC Medicine* 16, no. 1 (2018): 219, https://doi.org/10.1186/s12916-018-1198-0.

38 Tanjaniina Laukkanen et al., "Association between Sauna Bathing and Fatal Cardiovascular and All-Cause Mortality Events," *JAMA Internal Medicine* 175, no. 4 (April 2015): 542–548, https://doi.org/10.1001/jamainternmed.2014.8187.

39 "Stroke Facts," U.S. Centers for Disease Control and Prevention, last modified October 14, 2022, https://www.cdc.gov/stroke/facts.htm.

40 Setor K. Kunutsor et al., "Sauna Bathing Reduces the Risk of Stroke in Finnish Men and Women: A Prospective Cohort Study," *Neurology* 90, no. 22 (May 2018): e1937–e1944, https://doi.org/10.1212/WNL.0000000000005606.

41 Katriina Kukkonen-Harjula et al., "Haemodynamic and Hormonal Responses to Heat Exposure in a Finnish Sauna Bath," *European Journal of Applied Physiology and Occupational Physiology* 58, no. 5 (1989): 543–550, https://doi.org/10.1007/BF02330710; J. Leppäluoto et al., "Endocrine Effects of Repeated Sauna Bathing," *Acta Physiologica Scandinavica* 128, no. 3 (November 1986): 467–470, https://doi.org/10.1111/j.1748-1716.1986.tb08000.x.

42 Minna L. Hannuksela and Samer Ellahham, "Benefits and Risks of Sauna Bathing," *The American Journal of Medicine* 110, no. 2 (2001): 118–126, https://doi.org/10.1016/S0002-9343(00)00671-9; Jari A. Laukkanen, Tanjaniina Laukkanen, and Setor K. Kunutsor, "Cardiovascular and Other Health Benefits of Sauna Bathing: A Review of the Evidence," *Mayo Clinic Proceedings* 93, no. 8 (August 2018): 1111–1121, https://doi.org/10.1016/j.mayocp.2018.04.008.

43 Matt Pappas, "How Cold Water Can Treat Depression, PTSD, and Improve Overall Mental Health," *Surviving My Past* (blog), March 12, 2018, https://www.survivingmypast.net/cold-water-can-treat-depression-ptsd-improve-overall-mental-health/.

44 Avni Bavishi, Martin D. Slade, and Becca R. Levy, "A Chapter a Day: Association of Book Reading with Longevity," *Social Science and Medicine* 164 (September 2016): 44–48, https://doi.org/10.1016/j.socscimed.2016.07.014.

45 Anne-Marie Chang et al., "Evening Use of Light-Emitting eReaders Negatively Affects Sleep, Circadian Timing, and Next-Morning Alertness," *Proceedings of the National Academy of Sciences of the United States of America* 112, no. 4 (December 2014): 1232–1237, https://doi.org/10.1073/pnas.1418490112.

46 Salman Akhtar, "Patience," *The Psychoanalytic Review* 102, no. 1 (February 2015): 93–122, https://doi.org/10.1521/prev.2015.102.1.93.

47 Michael Rosholm, Mai Bjørnskov Mikkelsen, and Kamilla Gumede, "Your Move: The Effect of Chess on Mathematics Test Scores," *PLoS One* 12, no. 5 (May 2017): e0177257, https://doi.org/10.1371/journal.pone.0177257.

48 Catherine Y. Wan and Gottfried Schlaug, "Music Making as a Tool for Promoting Brain Plasticity across the Life Span," *The Neuroscientist* 16, no. 5 (2010): 566–577, https://doi.org/10.1177/1073858410377805.

49 Anne Bolwerk et al., "How Art Changes Your Brain: Differential Effects of Visual Art Production and Cognitive Art Evaluation on Functional Brain Connectivity," *PLoS One* 9, no. 7 (2014): e101035, https://doi.org/10.1371/journal.pone.0101035.

www.ingramcontent.com/pod-product-compliance
Lightning Source LLC
Chambersburg PA
CBHW030511080526
44586CB00011B/152